A People's Guide to

AN INTERFAITH
CHRISTIAN THEOLOGY

In a Time of

TRANSFORMATION

A People's Guide to

AN INTERFAITH
CHRISTIAN THEOLOGY

In a Time of

TRANSFORMATION

Harvey H. Honig, PhD

SHANTI ARTS PUBLISHING
BRUNSWICK, MAINE

A People's Guide to
an Interfaith Christian Theology
In a Time of Transformation

Copyright © 2022 Harvey H. Honig, PhD

Published by Shanti Arts Publishing

Cover design by SCHEDLER BRENNAN design + consulting

Cover image: *The Angel of 5th Realisation*
by Dimitra Natskouli and used with her permission

Interior design by Shanti Arts Designs

Shanti Arts LLC
193 Hillside Road
Brunswick, Maine 04011
shantiarts.com

Printed in the United States of America

THE HOLY BIBLE, NEW INTERNATIONAL VERSION®,
NIV® Copyright © 1973, 1978, 1984, 2011 by Biblica, Inc.™
Used by permission. All rights reserved worldwide.

Translation of the Aramaic Lord's Prayer copyright Neil
Douglas-Klotz 2011 from *Desert Wisdom: A Nomad's Guide
to Life's Big Questions from the Heart of the Native Middle East.*
ARC Books. Abwoon Network. https://abwoon.org

ISBN: 978-1-956056-33-4 (softcover)
ISBN: 978-1-956056-34-1 (ebook)

Library of Congress Control Number: 2022937825

There are many people in my life who have supported me during this time of writing and would be deserving of a dedication. However, this book is dedicated to you, all the future readers of this book, who are the reason for this book, and to the transformation of consciousness that is occurring.

IN MEMORIAM

This book is also dedicated to the memory of Fred Gustafson, a friend and colleague who supported this work by his enthusiastic encouragement as well as by his example as a writer.

CONTENTS

ACKNOWLEDGMENTS

THERE ARE MANY FRIENDS AND HELPERS IN ADDITION TO THOSE acknowledged in the cover credits, and this book would have not been written without their help and support. However, at a deeper level I want to acknowledge that this book provides no original scholarship but brings together the ideas of scholars that have helped us to understand this tradition in light of current biblical, cultural, and psychological understanding. Anything original or creative is in the integration of knowledge studied on a much deeper level by the scholars mentioned in the body of this book as well as that given by the many teachers who have shaped my knowledge and understanding, and my own personal experience as outlined in this book. For any readers who are interested, I would be happy to reply to questions about my sources or to suggest other resources for reading that might be of interest.

PREFACE

❧

I OFFER THIS WORK OUT OF MY OWN LIFE AND EXPERIENCE. I grew up within the framework of conservative Christianity and became a Lutheran minister but needed to have a more spacious framework than that which shaped so much of my life. I explored and experienced other paths of religion and spirituality but in the recent years of my life found that the message, mission, and being of Jesus were very powerful and transformative. I resonated with the process that Houston Smith describes in his autobiography about his own journey.1

However, because the life of Jesus is embedded within a whole biblical and historical framework, I wanted to share some of the recent knowledge that gives more meaning and makes more sense within the framework of our current world. I wanted to create a theological framework which followed the traditional Christian sources of knowledge but was written for other seekers who were drawn to the being and message of Jesus but could no longer relate to the dissonance between reality and belief that so many churches required.

This theology is similar to traditional Christian theologies in that it draws on the traditional sources—i.e., scripture, historical interpretation, natural law (which for much of the history of the church and for me means science)—and direct experience. It also follows the traditional tripartite division of God and Creation, Jesus and Redemption, and Holy Spirit and Sanctification. (I have changed the term Sanctification to Transformation for reasons I explain in the book.)

In two ways it is dissimilar to traditional Christian theology: First, it is aimed, as the title implies, at all people who are searching to understand and make sense of this tradition rather than an academic or scholarly audience or one from a specific denominational framework. Second, it views Christianity as a way of framing this knowledge, rather than as the only or true way.

This is, of course, not totally new. Many writers in the Christian tradition now view their work within an interfaith context. Paul Tillich's *Systematic Theology*[2] was written as a Christian theology, but he believed the future theologies would be interfaith rather than specifically Christian.[3]

I agree with Tillich and many others that the time is past for viewing Christian theology as the only way to frame our knowledge about God. Nevertheless, I also believe, as he did, that this tradition can be meaningful for our time and that there is still reason to view Christianity in its essence as relevant today. However, it needs to be understood in the light of current cultural, social, and scientific knowledge, as all forms of knowledge need to be understood within the context of current knowledge.

In light of this new vision, we no longer can have a fragmented view of theological or any other reality. We live in a time when our perspective on reality has been radically impacted by the view of our world from outer space. This shift has been visual and metaphorical rather than logical and verbal. Consequently, in my reformulation of theology I use the metaphor of Spaceship Earth to highlight the necessity of a unitary and inclusive story to help save our planet. This metaphor defines and shapes the age that is now emerging, and it is in all of Spaceship Earth that the Holy Spirit is at work today.

AN INTEGRAL
CHRISTIAN THEOLOGY

Why I Wrote This Book

I WAS RECENTLY STRUCK BY A QUOTATION FROM TONI
Morrison: "If there is a book that you would like to read,
but it hasn't been written yet, then you must write it."4

The book I want to read is one that speaks to thoughtful
spiritual seekers who are searching for a meaningful, coherent
approach to religion. Because of my history and background,
I want to write primarily within the context of the Christian
framework that is part of my background and the cultural
framework of most people in the United States, Canada, and
much of Europe. However, I want to write for those who
understand that the spiritual search is not a search for the
ultimate truth but a way to speak about God, the spiritual path,
and religion in a way that is meaningful today and addresses
contemporary problems and challenges. I want to read a
book that is intellectually compatible with science and other
measures of reality as we know them today, yet does not limit its
theological viewpoint to a rational, intellectual approach but is
open to the transcendent and mystical dimensions of existence.

There are many writers and books that address these
issues and speak to the contemporary Christian seeker. I have
benefited from many of these writers but have not found in
them the integrative approach that I seek.

As I was thinking about this process and feeling some
sense of calling to respond to this need, I came across the above
quotation from Toni Morrison, which intensified my sense of
calling. I must write it? That seemed quite a challenge. Her

words truly did add the spark to my process, but these writings, these reflections about theology have evolved over a lifetime of learning, experience, and reflection. When I began writing, I believed that the combination of my age—seventy-seven—my own long spiritual search, and my study in theology and psychology could offer a way of understanding and integrating this background that would be useful to seekers today. My journey (see below) to this point in my theological reflections has been a long and somewhat meandering journey, but I have explored many paths in the course of finding my own spiritual path.

What Does Theology Mean Today?

Theology is not a word that communicates meaningfully to most people today. Too often, we have experienced theology as a word for dogmatic formulations that express the "one true description of divine reality"—as if there could be any true description of divine reality, any more than there can be any one true description of material and scientific reality. We have only the ongoing attempt to shape our descriptions as closely as we can to reality as we know it through various sources.

Theologies of the past have often been divisive and imbued with a sense of possessing the truth. The last great formulation of Protestant Christianity was written by Paul Tillich[5] who was the foremost Protestant theologian of his time—the middle of the last century. He provided a bridge from a traditional Christian theology to one that spoke to his time and culture. He helped shift our view of God from a personal being in charge of the universe to what he called the Ground of Being, meaning a shift to understanding God as that basic inner and outer source of being.

Theology is not a popular concept in our time, and in the past, it often was framed as *our theology* versus *your theology*. In my book, theology is simply another word for our attempts to put into words the meaning of various encounters with the divine. There is no one right theology; there are only the various fingers pointing at the moon. Nevertheless, it is important to see that moon that we call God as clearly as possible and to formulate our knowledge of God in various theologies as accurately as possible in light of what we currently know, experience, and feel.

Theology always grows out of a movement begun by its founder based on a profound encounter with the divine. The power of the original religious experience is transmitted directly to the original followers and over time is conveyed to future followers by words, experiences, and rituals that eventually are codified into an institutional framework and become dogma. For example, in the case of Christianity, the original encounter and transformative experience of Jesus with the Divine was directly shared with his followers. They did not see themselves as founders of Christianity, but were sharing their own transformative experience, which became a movement simply called the Way. The earliest follower to begin to shape the story in written form was the apostle Paul, who began to shape his own profound mystical experience of Jesus in a way that could appeal to people living in the world of Graeco-Roman culture.[6] This was the beginning of a "Christian Theology", which later became codified and dogmatic as it became more institutional.

Theology as Perennial Philosophy

Earlier in my life, I was granted the privilege of spending some fairly intimate time with Huston Smith, the interfaith scholar who opened our Western world to the awareness of the beauty and truth of other religions. He demonstrated that at their highest level of understanding and development, all advanced religions pointed to a very similar moon. I first heard the term *perennial philosophy* from Huston Smith, which he described as the tradition that understands that the core truths at the heart of each expression of the great world religions are very similar.[7]

Paul Tillich recognized that his three-volume *Systematic Theology* would be the last to define specific Christian theologies and that future theologies would be more inclusive and universal.[8]

It is my conviction that we can no longer believe in a theology that purports to describe a system of objective reality. However, we can make an attempt to expand on a particular finger pointing at the moon. From time immemorial, humans have attempted to describe their experience of the divine, as scientists have attempted to describe their experience of material reality.

The Meaning of God Today

I use the parallel with scientific work consciously because I believe that the term *God* no longer can have any specific content but is only our term to describe the underlying nature of reality as experienced though the lens of religious experience. I also recognize that even using the term *God* is fraught with danger because for so many people, the term carries emotional baggage that can turn off any further attempt to communicate about our experience of the divine. Theology is often understood in terms of right/wrong, us/them beliefs, when in truth the underlying nature of the divine, as of all reality, is unitary. However, while the essential nature of the divine is unitary, the human experience and description of the divine is a rich tapestry of beliefs shaped by profound experiences, and each strand of the tapestry makes up the whole.

The Role of Belief Today

So why try to describe the finger pointing at the moon? Why does it matter what we believe? We are living in a paradoxical moment in history in terms of our reaction to beliefs. On the one hand, for many people there is a negative reaction against any institutional form of belief and an emphasis on each person's right to their own beliefs. On the other hand, in both psychology and New Age thinking, we see a renewed understanding of how much our lives are shaped by our beliefs and how much our beliefs create our reality. Scientists are also increasingly realizing that even their "objective" methods are subject to observer bias and interference.[9]

I do not believe that our beliefs create reality. Whether we are defining divine reality or scientific reality, there is an objective reality that is larger than our little minds and beyond the capacity of our instruments to measure it. However, our beliefs both shape our response to reality—whether divine or scientific—and in turn affect our perception of reality.

Because of this objective and subjective nature of our reality, it is very important not only that our beliefs correspond as accurately as possible to objective reality but also are accurate reflections of our inner experience.

I understand why there is so much negative reaction against the concept of belief and a corresponding attempt to separate belief from faith. The terms *belief* and *faith*, like the term *God*, carry a great deal of emotional baggage from the attempts to claim and codify the content of those terms, and to demonize the beliefs of others. The history of Christianity is certainly a history of the negative and destructive power of belief systems, as well as the positive and creative power of belief/faith.

The Movement from Belief as Faith to Belief as Dogma

As earliest Christianity moved from belief as an aspect of faith that the Kingdom of God had arrived and that Jesus's life was one of transcendence rather than failure to the post-Nicaean world after Christianity (second half of the second century through the fourth century), it became increasingly systematized into a dogmatic theology rather than a group of different stories with varying descriptions of the meanings of those stories. Prior to that time, there were various gospel traditions that existed as parallel fingers pointing at the moon of the reality of the encounter with Jesus and his life. The tragic result of this focus on the one and only truth was that more Christians were killed by other Christians during that post-Nicaean period over competing Christian theologies than ever had been killed by the Romans.[10] The Council of Nicaea unleashed a devastating internecine conflict among Christians and conflated belief with power. The Church was in effect taken over by the Roman Empire and its power and domination model. In this model, only one way and one belief were allowed, and the Church and the Roman Empire became inseparable.

Knowing this history, I have no illusions about the negative aspects of belief and orthodoxy. However, because the bathwater of the accumulation of power and domination theology is so bloody and murky, I do not want to throw out the baby with the bathwater; I want to recognize that the bathwater must be as clean and pure as possible, and constantly changed to conform to changing reality.

What Are My Qualifications? What Are My Sources?

The above questions may well occur to you, my reader, at this point. Addressing my qualifications first, as of this writing, I am a seventy-seven-year-old white male who has been on a long journey of spiritual and personal searching for what is the most true and real way of understanding my world. Whether it is the world of religion and the spirit, the inner world of experience understood through psychology/analysis, or the world of scientific reality, which continues to shift and become more amazing and complex, these are all part of the one reality that I have studied.

The traditional sources for Christianity have been scripture, tradition, direct experience, and natural law, which has always meant the most current scientific and philosophical understanding of the world in which we live. Those sources are certainly central for me, but I want to draw on all knowledge available to me about both our scientific/material reality and the various ways we currently understand our experience of divine/human reality.

A Brief Review of My Life and Experience

I started life in a remote town in rural Canada where my father was a conservative Lutheran minister in a community of German immigrants. Much of my early life was lived within the constricted framework of a very narrow and dogmatic religion, which also restricted my exposure to and understanding of the natural world in which I lived. To my father and those who shared his beliefs, science and reason were dangerous and to be avoided. I remained in that framework through my teens, and following the only road readily available within that belief system, I became a conservative Lutheran minister.

Our Lutheran ministerial system of education was relatively conservative and restricted, but also rather scholarly, and we were given some tools of scholarship that at least opened us to other possibilities. I did encounter a few minds, like those of Martin Marty and Jaroslav Pelikan, that were educated within that system but moved beyond it to allow them to become recognized scholars.[11]

At the end of my seminary years, I was given an opportunity to study at the Oberlin School of Theology where my world began to open up in a theological and psychological sense. I was introduced to the psychology of Carl Jung and the theology of Paul Tillich and received a master's degree in the theology of pastoral counseling. Both Jung and Tillich gave me tools to expand my inner world and to open up the search for a more true and expansive religious framework. After serving for five years as a minister, I realized that my world of understanding had expanded to the point that I could no longer work within that narrow theological framework and worldview, and left the parish ministry. I had become more attracted to my personal need to heal and understand my inner world. Jung helped me understand and access more of my inner world and gave me tools for further searching. Subsequently, I became convinced that this search for inner truth and healing was the ministry most needed in today's world.

At that point, in 1968, I moved to Chicago and began Jungian analysis with Dr. June Singer. Over the next few years, I participated in the formative years of Jungian analytic training in Chicago and enrolled in a Ph.D. program in psychology at Loyola University Chicago. In 1979 I received a diplomate accrediting me as a Jungian analyst and a Ph.D. recognizing me as a psychologist.

Those years between 1963, when I graduated from seminary and went to Oberlin, to 1979, when I graduated as an analyst and psychologist, were years of transformative change, not only for me, personally, but for our country. It was an era of black people reclaiming their rights as humans, and at Oberlin I was given the opportunity to meet seminal figures such as Martin Luther King and the powerful singer Odetta, and to participate in a march on Washington of engaged clergymen and others. Those were also the years of inner experimentation and revolution through mind-altering substances as well as years of revolt against our political system, followed by years of retrenchment and suppression.

While my wife and I were camping on Cape Cod in the summer of 1968 during our transition to Chicago, we happened to see that a TV set from a neighboring campsite was flashing images from the Democratic Convention in Chicago. These vivid images showed the conflict between the police, who were carrying out the divide and control policies given them by the city establishment and embodied by Mayor Daley, and the protesters. I realized that I was moving to the heart of our cultural conflict.

By then I was moving away from religion and no longer went to church. If anyone had asked, I would have called myself an agnostic. I was also going through personal turmoil as a result of the shift in my beliefs and the dissonance that shift created for my still conservative parents. However, my encounter with the personal and collective unconscious in Jungian analysis was beginning to show me that at those levels, some elements of space/time reality did not fit within our narrow framework of material reality. This understanding led me back into a connection with a spiritual, if not religious, search for truth and meaning.

In my lifelong search for the expression of that spiritual meaning, I have explored Sufism and Buddhism, among other paths. The Sufi path was helpful for me in its openness to mystical experience of all faiths and the connection with the Divine Beloved. The Buddhist path gave me many tools for dealing with suffering, such as focusing on the proper relationship with mind and practicing meditation.

These experiences have confirmed for me the multilayered nature of spiritual/religious truth and practice, and demonstrated that true practitioners from all major religious traditions at the highest level of understanding have more in common than do conventionally religious people of any single faith tradition.

However, it is also clear that both Sufism and Buddhism have functioned very well without a theology as such. They have, rather, given us tools to connect with the divine (Sufism) and deal with the suffering created by our minds in our response to reality (Buddhism).

Many people have provided me with spiritual sustenance along the way, and this theology incorporates material from many current spiritual and scientific thinkers. As stated in the preface, although this is not an academic or scholarly work, I will refer to important influences along the way and will append a list of various writers and books that could provide further reading. I am attempting to integrate a great deal of current knowledge, and I acknowledge that this project is somewhat a case of a fool rushing in where angels fear to tread.

Is There Really a Need for This Book Today?

I wrote this book because there have been so many intelligent writers and thinkers who have given us ways of reflecting on different aspects of the Christian faith that are more in touch with reality as we know it currently. I believe that these thinkers need to be integrated into current religious thinking in a more approachable and widespread way. Writers from Christian and other religious traditions are integrating our current knowledge of evolution and our greater and more accurate understanding of the structure of the world. There is a whole world of biblical scholarship that helps us understand the scriptures in their original context. There are many pastoral applications of current theological and psychological insights. However, there is not, to my knowledge, an attempt to update and integrate our current state of knowledge about God in an easily accessible manner.

One of the best of the current pastoral commentators, Richard Rohr, points out that the purpose of religion is transformation and participation in the divine nature. He states that "You become the God you worship."[12] Martin Luther said, *Wie man glaubt, so ist er* ("as a man believes, so he is"[13]). Psychology has helped us understand that our core beliefs shape our lives. If our beliefs have that much impact on our relationship to the divine, to our daily reality, and to who we are, it is important that they reflect our current understanding of religious and scientific truth as accurately as possible.

Even more important for religion is the requirement that our beliefs transform us. This is the measure that Jesus gave to his disciples. When they approached Jesus with the concern that other teachers would come along claiming false beliefs, Jesus said they would know whether these future teachers were of the Spirit by their fruits, by their being consistent with the Spirit, which he would send to them. Paul also said that the fruits of the Spirit are love, joy, and peace. If our beliefs do not produce love, joy, and peace, they are not truly of Christ and of the Spirit.

Additionally, I wrote this book to challenge the naive and infantile form of faith that dominates so much of Christianity today. If these beliefs had no larger impact than on the personal lives of those who believe them, I would simply call it a case of live and let live. However, these immature beliefs have impacted the public sphere to the point that the increasing split between revealed knowledge and scientific thinking is threatening to destroy our world as we ignore climate change. In this case, immature beliefs are like the leaders of the Titanic urging people to trust that God will save them rather than taking action to avoid the iceberg; in any case, they will all be going to a better place in the sky. Many Christians have confused the invitation of Jesus to become as a child with immature and childish versions of Christianity. Jesus demanded nothing less than a mature faith, and he challenged the naive and simplistic beliefs of the religious leaders of his time.

What is a mature faith? The Franciscan writer Richard Rohr describes mature faith beautifully and succinctly in *Falling Upward*. This book was given to me by a friend shortly before I began this project and gives as good a definition of mature Christianity as I have found. Mature Christianity moves beyond childish dependence to co-creation with God and thus with evolution. It moves from helplessness to a sense of personal responsibility and participation in the healing of our planet. It moves from a narrow definition of God that must be protected from scientific reality and the dangers of the "modern world" to an understanding that however we understand the term *God*, it is larger than any of our little belief systems and as present in the modern world as at any time in history.

Finally, I wrote this book because I felt called to write it. It seems to my rational mind a dubious and overwhelming task, but what I think makes no difference to the larger Self. The value of being an Elder is that what the ego thinks it wants becomes less relevant as we mature, and what our creative self wants—the Self that is an expression of the divine spirit—becomes central. That is why in response to this inner call, I offer a more mature and universal understanding of the Christian faith for our time.

PART ONE

GOD AND CREATION

Why God as Trinity?

IN MY OWN INDOCTRINATION INTO CHRISTIANITY, GOD WAS presented in the form of a Trinity: God the Father/ Creator, God the Son/Redeemer, and God the Holy Spirit/Sanctifier.

As I reached adulthood and was exposed to wider sources of Christianity, I no longer thought of this concept as a literal description of God. In fact, the concept of a Trinity no longer held meaning or relevance for me, and no literal attempt to define the nature of God was meaningful. It seemed to me that anyone who claimed to define God in this moment in history did not really know God. As I read the Christian mystics and current biblical scholars, I found that no definition of God could describe the full reality of the experience of the divine. Anyone who responsibly uses the term *God* today, does it with a great deal of hesitation and apology for all the distortions of reality, the wars over the claim to the true God, and the use of the idea of God to control and punish. Anyone who has truly experienced connection with the divine mystery through mystical experience cannot define this experience. It is a reality beyond words and ideas, a profound expression of the divine encounter that has transformed the lives of those who have experienced it.

While we cannot define or encapsulate God, we need a word for the idea that there is an ultimate reality that religious people have experienced in a form that has powerfully affected their lives, a reality that humans have called God.

An Understanding of the Concept of Trinity

For me, it no longer made sense to talk about God in three persons—as though God could be expressed in any personhood outside of the personal form that Jesus and other avatars manifested and that we all can experience in a personal relationship with the nature of divinity. However, we can talk about God in three manifestations. God is traditionally known through creation and nature. God is also known through avatars or powerful expressions of the fullness of divine being. In Christianity, this is manifested in Jesus, seen to be such a full embodiment of God that he was considered divine. Lastly, God is experienced as the pervading divine energy, which in the Western tradition has been identified as: *Ruach*, the Hebrew word for breath; *Pneuma*, the Greek word for breath; and *Psyche*, the Greek word for spirit. These words point to an aspect of the divine that is present and active in the world, that is as close to us as our breath, or as the life force present in each of us.[14] (For a scholarly contemporary presentation of the trinitarian nature of the divine, see Cynthia Bourgeault, *The Holy Trinity*.) In the Eastern tradition, this form of divine energy is most often known as *prana* or *kundalini* energy to denote that energetic aspect of underlying reality that we can access through our breath or other means.

Throughout this book, I will continue to draw on this traditional triune expression of the meaning of God in Christianity, not as a literal description of the essence of God but as a way of understanding and reflecting on our experience of the divine.

Trinity or Quaternity?

One of my primary teachers, Carl Jung, the famous Swiss

psychoanalyst, often attempted to provide a complementary view to that of mainstream Christianity. He suggested that we need to expand the Trinity to a Quaternity.[15] When Jung talked about religion, he was speaking not so much theologically as psychologically. What Jung accurately intuited is the missing element of the feminine in our experience of the divine, which he added as the fourth element of the divinity. In my view, he was right in his intuition that an unbalanced masculine image of the divine has needed the completion of the feminine. However, the nature of the Trinity is itself neither masculine nor feminine but is beyond gender. It has become important to me and to most progressive contemporary Christian thinkers, to understand and emphasize that the term *God* is not a patriarchal or masculine term.

The source of these gendered references is the fact that as we experience the divine as humans, we have often attributed gender characteristics to this experience. Creation itself is not a masculine activity, and the earliest creator gods were feminine. The third/active aspect of the divinity was often personified as Sophia—divine wisdom—especially in the Wisdom literature.[16] Ultimately, the essence of this Trinitarian formulation is that our conception of God is relational and dynamic, continuing even now to create, redeem, and transform.

Sources of Our Ideas about God: The Bible

The Judeo-Christian understanding of God is expressed in the Bible. Anyone reading the Bible without preconceptions recognizes that it cannot be a literal description of historical and physical reality because it contains internal contradictions and multilayered descriptions of what its writers understood their physical world to be. Recent scholars have helped us understand that as biblical writings evolved, they reflected a great deal of development in their level of consciousness and understanding. Rather than presenting one unified story, the biblical accounts incorporated varying theological viewpoints that led to differing biblical accounts of creation and the history of the world in the Old Testament.[17]

The Bible is not written as a scientific book or as a literal description of how creation occurred. It is a book that contains deep truth. However, this is not the truth of an objective history or a literal account of how the world came to be. It is in its essence a deep truth about the relationship between God and humans. For instance, the Bible contains descriptions of divine/human encounters that in the earliest instances, such as in the story of Adam and Eve, are more symbolic and archetypal than historical.[18] Later encounters, such as that of God calling Abraham to leave his native home and begin a new nation, seem to be a mixture of history and legend. In each instance, these encounters became part of the history of a group of tribes that became the nation of Israel. They became significant in the history of our Judeo-Christian world precisely because of this relationship and how it became recorded in their collective sacred writings that later became the Old Testament. They thus became the history of the divine/human relationship for all of us in that tradition, the description of the origins and the stories containing our shared religious tradition.

Our current understanding of the Bible, at least among those scholars who study it more objectively, is that it is not meant to be taken literally or as a scientific statement about reality. It is rather a story of creation, of fall and redemption (or separation and relationship), and of transformation. These elements pervade the Old and New Testaments.

This understanding of the true purpose of the Bible frees us from needing God as an explanatory principle, as a philosophical first cause. Evolution does not require anything beyond itself any more than the operation of DNA requires a higher intelligence. These are simply the mechanisms by which the process of life unfolds.

Knowledge from Creation/Nature/Science

When we behold the wonder of creation, we can ask the question: How did this come to be? This is an important question that has prompted humans to seek to understand the nature of reality. One of the ways of understanding reality is through science. Insofar as science is a description of physical reality as we understand it today, there is no conflict between the description of reality as provided through science and reality understood through religion.

One way of understanding our belief in a creator God is seeing that nature is not designed to fool us or take us away from the divine. It simply requires a constant enlargement and reformulation of our understanding of our physical world. This has always been true, as evidenced by the way the description of God evolves in the Old Testament and our growing understanding that the biblical cosmology was based on a conception of the world as a tripartite, three-story universe—heaven, earth, and underworld.[19] In another significant shift from the biblical understanding of the universe, we have corrected our heliocentric and earth-centered universe to reflect our understanding of our true place in the cosmos.

Just as science struggles to shift to new paradigms as new discoveries about reality occur, we also struggle with changing paradigms as our understanding of God and the nature of religion evolves. Unfortunately, religion frequently becomes identified with its role as preserver of particular formulations of truth rather than as the living, evolving story of the divine reality breaking into our human reality. God is not now, and never has been, an intellectual proposition. The term *God* gives us a way of talking about our experiences of reverence, of presence, and of relationship with this divine reality. Those experiences can now, as easily as ever, be gifted to us through nature, whenever we experience that wonder and unity that comes when we let go of our small, egocentric selves and immerse ourselves in the ultimate wonder of being a part of nature. It can also be experienced through nature as examined through science, which created a sense of awe in Galileo, Newton, Einstein, and many others.

Our experiences of awe and wonder can be even more transcendent today as we peer through multiple lenses that have profoundly affected our awareness of the universe. For example, one such lens is evolution, which allows us to understand that all of the known universe evolved from one singular event over some fourteen billion years of unfolding life, a process so precise and intricate that it inspires wonder and amazement. This evolution story was connected in our time to the unfolding of the divine story by Teilhard de Chardin[20] and is elaborated today by such varied figures as Brian Swimme, Thomas Berry, Michael Dowd, and Barbara Marx Hubbard, among others. These are people who understand science and evolution, and are able to show in great detail how the acceptance of evolution is not a cause for distress and alienation for mature Christians, but a story about an incredibly intricate world.

The reality is that the more deeply and completely we see and understand nature, the more we experience the feelings of awe and amazement that we experience in the presence of the divine. Peering through the lens of the Hubble Telescope and other instruments of modern astronomy, we see that life is more varied and immense than our ancestors could have dreamed. Through the lens of the electron microscope, we see the wonders of DNA, our chromosomal structure, and the insect world. Through the lens of quantum reality, we glimpse a tiny section of a curtain pulled back to view a universe that is beyond our current level of understanding and description. This universe is so amazing in its tantalizing possibilities of multiple realities—presented to us in the last half century through string theory, the concept of particles and waves, the idea of nonlocal interactions—that like Einstein, Bohr, and more recent physicists, we experience awe and wonder. Whether we relate these experiences to that which we call God or see them as simply independent manifestations of the evolutionary process, they are all one reality, a reality that creates in us the same sense of awe and wonder that has characterized religious experience.

The Unlimited Sources of Knowledge of God

Our understanding of God is a rich tapestry that involves much more than the Bible and creation. For the Judeo-Christian world, the Bible is our story, our literature, our account of the developing old and new covenants between God and man. It is a repeating story of our creation, our falling away, our redemption, and our new life. And science is, for our Western developed world, as much a source of wonder as the world of nature has been for all humans over time.

But these are not the only sources of our understanding of the divine. The sources of our understanding are as unlimited as the many forms of creative expression giving us varied glimpses of reality: poetry, art, literature, dance, music, drumming, journeying, entheogenic (literally, mind-altering substances that birth God in us) experiences. There are also many other experiences through which transformative reality breaks into our lives. If God is the depth beneath all reality, it is this God that is at the heart of all depths.[21]

Furthermore, the God that we know through the Bible and Jesus Christ has, in the words of St Paul and others, been known at many times and places.[22] To cite a couple of examples, the Upanishads—sacred writings from Hinduism—and the Tao Te Ching are other windows to knowledge of the divine/ human story through which many people view ultimate reality.

The Role of Direct Experience

But perhaps the most important source of our knowledge of God throughout human history is that of direct experience. The church, as conveyor and "protector" of divine revelation, has been distrustful of direct experience, and there is reason for this distrust. Direct experience of the divine that has no symbolic container can be shattering and overwhelming.[23] If the voice we hear or the experience we have is a purely individual voice or experience with no connection to the larger Self (or the Holy Spirit), it can be a destructive voice rather than one that leads to love, joy, and peace. It can lead to tragic and misguided acts, such as Jonestown, or to the inflated experience of some who claim to speak for God.

At the same time, the direct experience of those who have truly connected with the divine or with the True Self that is not distorted by the ego or inflation is what allows the life of the church and the world to be renewed. Direct mystical experiences have been critical throughout the history of Christianity, from St. Paul to St. Francis, Catherine of Siena, Hildegarde of Bingen, and the whole tradition of Christian mystics. A tremendous hunger for that kind of connection still exists today, whether through poets like Rumi or through a return to and connection with mystical and contemplative religion. Outside the Christian tradition, we find a similar longing to experience connection with the divine through shamanic experiences or Eastern practices and/or gurus, as well as through entheogenic experiences. Searching people today often find more spiritual sustenance in those kinds of experiences than in formal religion. Similarly, in psychology, many of us hunger for practices that allow us to get in touch with the True Self, the deeper Self, the Self that calls us to personal renewal.

Since direct experience is often connected with the active element of the divine, the Holy Spirit, I will talk more of that connection in the third section about the Holy Spirit.

Themes of the Creation Narrative

I now want to return to the theme of creation/redemption/ transformation as narrated in the early Bible. There are several subthemes within the creation narrative. One is that we are created out of nothing, out of emptiness, out of (the Hebrew term) *Tohuvabohu*, translated in the King James version as "without form and void."[24] This view conveys that early shared awareness within spiritual traditions that we emerge from emptiness into form and that form and emptiness are one, which is also the view in Buddhism and contemporary physics. There is a constant transformation of matter and energy within all manifested reality.

Another subtheme is that we are created in the "image and likeness of God."[25] What does that mean? It means that as our images of the divine evolve and become more clear and whole, we evolve and become more clear and whole. As the Franciscan Richard Rohr phrases it, "You become the

God you worship." He goes on to say that the "Principle of Likeness" means that like knows like, love in me knows love. If there's no love in you, if you are filled with fear and hatred, you will not know God. You actually can't. There's no abiding place for an infinite God in you because your field is too small and safe. The infinite cannot abide inside the finite unless the finite is somehow released from its small boundaries and attracted outward into a larger field. Worshiping the true God is important not because there is a true and false God, but because it is important that we worship a God large enough to draw us toward truth and love.[26] This is the only way the concept of a "True God" has any meaning.

Why Differing Creation Stories and Differing Names for God?

From the beginning of the account in Genesis, there is no one consistent agreement about what creation is or what God is. Instead of one single narrative, different creation narratives are woven together, and the earliest names for God, such as *Elohim* and *El Shaddai* and others, seem to link back to earlier Canaanitic names for God, perhaps incorporating images of nature, of multiplicity. Scholars disagree about the origins and meaning of these various names. The name that comes to be used, *Jahweh*, which we know as *Jehovah*, originally denoted a "God among Gods," and over the development of time, it becomes first the "exalted God," then "the only true God."[27]

Mythological Rather than Literal Understanding

The relevance of this scholarship is the understanding that in the Old Testament, ideas about God emerge from ancient history and from shared experience, and evolve into the idea of the One God. Understanding this story is not about having the correct name or the correct ideas about God and creation since there is an evolving multiplicity in both the stories about creation and the ideas of the divine rather than one correct name or story. Nevertheless, some central themes emerge over these stories. In my view as well as that of most modern scholars, these themes carry more meaning when they are viewed mythologically than if we view them literally. Today, many people are beginning to understand that when we say mythical, we do not mean untrue. What we mean is that the message conveyed in the mythical is universal and timeless, beyond the realm of everyday literal truth. It is important to realize that because these ideas are presented in mythological form, they communicate not only to our conscious mind, but to our unconscious and experiential understanding, transcending the limits of time and place.[28]

If we look to Genesis as a literal account of creation, we can only see it as a time-bound and limited story from another era. However, if we understand that Genesis, like almost all biblical literature, is written to understand and present timeless truths in mythological and theological form, this book can speak to us very powerfully today. The names (as denoted in the original Hebrew) *Adam* (mankind) and *Eve* (living, mother of life) lend themselves to a symbolic and mythological understanding. They take us beyond the question of whether they were really the first humans to the question: What do these stories mean in the whole narrative of creation, divine/human encounter, fall, and redemption? This is the way Jesus treated these stories. When church leaders of his time quoted these early stories to trap him with true/false questions, he pointed beyond their literalism to the question of the divine-human relationship, to the symbolic meaning of Adam and Eve in the story of love and redemption.[29]

Mythological Views of the Fall

My own view of the story of the Fall is that it, like the story of Cain and Abel, takes place against the backdrop of emergent agrarian and urban cultures and the evolution of written language and left-brain dominance.[30] Humans were evolving from the hunter-gatherer cultures, which were much more unitary in consciousness, into more urban and agrarian cultures. Nature began to be experienced as something outside of us, something to be dominated and controlled. The serpent, a universal symbol of nature and often a central part of goddess worship, was no longer something that the urban cultures were connected to in the same primal way. These ancestors gained a great deal of knowledge and consciousness but lost their primal sense of unity and connection with all living beings. There are writers today who develop this idea that we went wrong when we made that shift and moved from an essential experience of unity and oneness with all being to an experience of alienation and competition.[31]

In traditional Christian theology, the Fall has always been an ambivalent symbol, sometimes called the *felix culpa*, the "fortunate mistake." After the Fall and the exclusion from the Garden of Eden, humans no longer lived in unitary consciousness, in harmony with all of nature, but were learning "good and evil."[32] We were learning to master nature, control nature, and begin the development of individual consciousness.

In its deepest sense, the mythological is beyond the categories of good or bad, as well as the limits of historical fact. It expresses the deeper reality unfolding. It takes a larger view of the historical and evolutionary forces that are emergent and connects them with the constant ongoing story of the relationship of the divine to the human. It is a story of an archetypal pattern of falling away, being called to relationship, and becoming part of the unfolding of the divine/human story. In that story, many of the central figures are not exemplary beings; in fact, they are very flawed, but they respond to the divine call, to the inner voice.

Cain and Abel can also be viewed as mythological rather than historical figures.[33] Trying to see them as historical figures defies logic, and many interpretations have been examples of strained attempts to fit them into a logical framework. However, if we see them as the representatives of the conflict between the agrarian and pastoral cultures, which their names and ways of life suggest, the story has meaning as a mythological condensation of an evolutionary process.

The Relevance of These Stories for Our Time

There is an awareness throughout this account of the Fall that the sense of individuality and the knowledge of good and evil come at the price of separation from nature and our original unity with God. This separation culminates in the Genesis narrative with the story of the Flood. This story is not unique to the Old Testament, in that there are other stories of a great flood, but in this context it describes that separation from the divine and from nature as being so extreme that it threatens the destruction of all animal and human life. Only one man, Noah, heeds the inner call to build an ark to preserve life. It is no accident that this story emerges in our time in movies and popular culture as a myth to which we can relate. Once again, our separation from and need to manipulate nature and other beings has led us to alienation from nature. It has severed us from a sense of connection with the consequences of this alienation that again threaten to bring about the destruction of much of life in its present form. Ironically, many people who claim to follow this biblical narrative appear to be the ones most separated from nature and from any sense of stewardship or need to preserve life in its current form. We are at a point when we need to create the equivalent of a symbolic ark that can survive the impact of our destructive relationship to nature.

The Relevance of Evolution for Our Time

We cannot go back and change the history of evolution and say the price of this Fall, this separation from nature, is too high for our civilization. We cannot change the emergence of the patriarchy, which also seems to be central to the Genesis narrative.[34] It is no more possible to change our evolutionary history than it is our personal history. However, as in our personal history, a crisis that threatens our survival forces us to confront the necessity of change. What we can do and what the divine voice in us constantly guides us to do, is move beyond our destructive relationship with nature and the feminine toward a unity of archetypal masculine and feminine and of science and nature. The concept of survival of the fittest is an inaccurate reading of evolution, an interpretation which Darwin himself warned us against.[35] Recent discoveries in evolutionary biology have informed us that what allowed the earliest humans to emerge as a species was cooperation and group intelligence.[36] Furthermore, the entire biblical narrative contradicts this idea of survival of the fittest. The chosen of God were not, for the most part, the strongest and the fittest, but those who responded to being called.

We are not called to go back to an earlier state before patriarchy, or when we lived in unity with nature. It is impossible to return to an earlier evolutionary stage. We are rather called to transcend the subjection of and control of nature and the feminine. We can understand and appreciate the religious knowledge of those who do live in harmony with nature and the earth rather than force on them a religion of domination and control. If we continue on this patriarchal pattern of alienation and separation, we endanger all life. In our current understanding of our relationship with God, biblically literate people no longer see events such as climate change as coming from a punishing God. Rather they are the result of our alienation from that sense of stewardship and care for all of life. This alienation has resulted in the imminent danger of causing our own extinction and the destruction of many other species. We have already destroyed much of nature and have altered our climate to the point of the prospect of another major life extinction.

Another important realization that we now understand through biblical scholarship and the historical record is that connecting the story of the Fall with the devil makes no sense. The idea of a devil/Satan did not emerge until late in the BCE, primarily in Zoroastrian culture. This is an idea inserted into the story from later ideas about Satan, after the time these early oral stories became part of the Old Testament. The other idea that people often connected with the story of the Fall is the idea of original sin. However, there was no such concept in the Old Testament.[37] St. Augustine and others saw original sin as prefigured in the Psalm attributed to David that talks about the heights and depths of human experience.[38] It poetically states that we are like the angels, but we are also caught in our darkness. This expression was never intended to be a theological statement, and it certainly was not an idea conveyed in the Genesis story.

Original Blessing Rather than Original Sin

The Genesis story, in fact, talks much more about Original Blessing. This theme has also been stated by Meister Eckhart[39] and is echoed by voices such as Matthew Fox[40] and Richard Rohr.[41] We were created in the image and likeness of God, and God was happy with the creation and continued to bless it.

What the story of the Fall communicates is that we no longer live in a state of unity with nature or with God but in a state of separation and individual consciousness. Because we have lost that original sense of unity, we are separated from the rest of the chain of being. Again, if taken literally, the idea that there was no death before Adam and Eve makes no sense. Evolution has included the process of death and rebirth from the very beginning. What makes sense mythologically and in reality is that the original state of oneness and connection with the divine was lost. This separation from the divine oneness of all being makes death no longer just a part of the ongoing river of life and death, but a tragic element of our individual and relational life. Even now among most indigenous cultures, death is experienced much more as simply part of life. Death is not a punishment for sin; it is a part of nature. However, sin is a word that refers in the Bible to that which separates us from the divine, from others, and from the rest of creation. That sense of separation does cause us to experience death as punishment and loss rather than as simply a part of the process of life unfolding.

That state of separation from God and nature is what required the development of laws and rules to govern societies in the ancient Near East, and the early Old Testament is certainly full of laws and rules. However, the rules proclaimed in that early Old Testament also included laws to promote justice and fairness, such as forgiveness of debts after seven years and the obligation of landowners to those who work the land.[42]

The Centrality of the Idea of Covenant

Another element in the Torah that was even more important than these early themes of creation and separation was the theme of the series of covenants, or agreements, between God and man. This is one of the central ideas of the Old Testament. Initially, there was the covenant with Noah that mankind would never again be destroyed. As a symbol of that promise, Noah and through him all mankind were given the sign of the rainbow. A central development of the covenant theme was the calling of Abraham to leave his people and his family and begin a new tribal dynasty, ritualized with the sign of circumcision. In the telling of the old story, this was the beginning of the agreement between God and his chosen people: Abraham and his descendants would worship the true God, and He would choose them as His people. (In this account it is a male god, although feminine and household images of God continued to exist.) This covenant was then renewed under Moses with the whole tribal group at Mount Sinai, and the descendants of Abraham, Isaac, and Jacob continued to be embraced as a chosen people. However, we know that, historically, circumcision did not begin with a historical Abraham. Evidence of circumcision goes back 15,000 years at least, and we have visual evidence that it occurred among the Egyptians.[43]

Nonetheless, in this Old Testament story, which is framed as God and His chosen people, circumcision is the sign of the special bond that exists between them. All of this "history" tells a story of a special relationship that existed prior to the laws and ritual prescriptions. Whatever the historical realities behind this story, it tells of this unique connection in which God calls Abraham, promising that he and his descendants will be as numerous as the stars.[44]

This agreement is not made because Abraham is especially virtuous. For instance, he denies that Sarah is his wife in the face of a threat from the Pharaoh; he does not believe that Sarah will really conceive in her old age, and he gets rid of his maidservant Hagar and her son Ishmael when Sarah tells him to after conceiving her own child. Much of this story does not hold up as a historical document, but that does not matter. The story becomes much more meaningful when understood as a symbolic and theological story of a relationship, which involves particular tribes that come to be known as Israel.

The story of this relationship begins in the universal, with Adam and Eve, and because they are symbolic representatives of mankind, the relationship is with all of humanity. After the separation, a special relationship is formed with Abraham and his descendants, which becomes the story of Israel, and thus, our story. It is a story of God choosing to relate with humanity, a story of a Fall and many forms of redemption in which imperfect humans are chosen. Thus, it becomes a universal story.

The Relationship of Covenant and Laws

It is this relationship between God and the chosen people that makes the history and the laws and ritual descriptions meaningful. God has chosen them to be his people, and they are to follow his commands.

One of the understandings that we have gained in psychology is that laws alienate when there is no relationship among the lawgivers, enforcers, and the people governed by the laws. In communities where people experience no sense of belonging, where there is no identification with the lawgivers and law preservers, laws do not protect us but rather alienate us. For example, in colonized communities, where the lawgivers and law preservers are institutions upholding that colonization, the colonized people experience police and other law enforcers as alien and dangerous rather than protective.[45] One of the great contributions of Old Testament theology is that these laws are seen within the context of God and God's people.

It is also true that this is a theological understanding that emerges much later in the biblical story and is inserted into the early narratives. This focus on the relationship reaches its height in the time of the prophets, that critical time in the divine human narrative of the Great Transformation, described by Karen Armstrong.[46] There is not any one theology or history that creates a unified story of man and the chosen people. There are a series of sometimes differing and competing mythohistorical accounts, and sometimes competing ways of understanding the relationship or differing theologies. As the understanding of the divine evolves, so does the understanding of the relationship between God and the chosen people.[47]

The Context and Origins of the Old Testament

Karen Armstrong has provided us a comprehensible and scholarly account of the development of the Old Testament as well as its relationship to other religious developments around that time in various parts of the world.[48] We know that the Old Testament documents began to be transcribed into written form sometime early in the Axial period, around 800 BCE. Prior to these written documents, there were oral traditions and various stories that were handed down from earlier periods, but in the time after 800 BCE, these written documents began to take the form that we know as the Pentateuch—a term used for the first five books of the Bible— or the Torah. These documents interweave various accounts and stories from that earlier period.

Karen Armstrong and the Axial Age

The Axial Age was a period of great turmoil and constantly shifting allegiances among the people of the Middle East, and this continued until the time of the Roman Empire. Israel was caught between the great powers of Assyria, Persia, and Egypt and was not in charge of its own destiny. During that period, culminating in their times of captivity, challenges arose to the traditional understanding of what it meant to worship the true God and be the chosen people. The Israelites could look back and idealize the time of Moses or the time of David and Solomon. But it was hard for them to continue to believe that the worship of the true God meant that they were more blessed in any temporal sense than those around them who worshiped other gods.

Two fundamental responses to this challenge to traditional ideas of God's blessing and the nature of good and evil emerged in the biblical literature. One response was the belief that these tragic events were happening because their faith or their rituals were not pure enough, and they were displeasing a very jealous and punitive God who demanded total obedience and loyalty as well as pure ritual worship. This theology was personified in the figure of Elijah, the great prophet, who had become a legendary figure among the tribes. Those who compiled the stories about Elijah during this period described an evolution of belief in Jahweh. Those with this belief held that it was no longer permissible to worship Jahweh as the supreme deity among other deities. It seems that in earlier history, the name Baal was used somewhat interchangeably as one of the divine names. By the time of Elijah, particularly after worship of Baal became connected with Jezebel, it was no longer permissible to worship Baal or to practice fertility rites, and the name Baal came to be viewed as the term for the false God. The implication of this was that these fertility rites connected with Baal continued to be practiced among many of the people, especially agricultural people. For this emerging theology personified by Elijah, there had to be pure worship of the only true God and belief that only He was all-powerful. Now the figures of Ahab, who had pursued strategic alliances to help preserve his people in the middle of the ongoing conflicts, and his wife Jezebel, became evil figures who represented the lack of belief in the only power of God.[49]

The Message of the Prophets

The second theological response was represented by the great prophets of this time, figures such as Hosea, Micah,

Amos, and Jeremiah, who viewed the captivities and other disastrous events occurring to God's chosen people as due to their failure to be true to the compassionate and merciful God who had called them into relationship. It is during this time that the image of God as lover, as one who calls his people as a husband calls his wife, emerged. This God wants justice and mercy, and it is the failure of his people to practice justice and mercy, to walk humbly with their God that has led to God's judgment, culminating in the destruction of the temple and the great captivity.[50]

The Message of the Book of Job

During this later period, there are also challenges to earlier theological beliefs about justice and punishment in the Book of Job. Job poses a challenge to the view, still current today, that good people are rewarded and bad people punished. This story is also obviously a mythological teaching story rather than a historical account, but its importance relates to the advancement it represents in the understanding of the nature of good and evil and its role in blessing and punishment. In this account, Job is a good, upright, and prosperous man. God is happy with him, seeing him as a man of faith. However, Satan—who is not a figure of evil but more like a devil's advocate to challenge consciousness—tells God that the only reason Job follows him is because of his prosperity, and that if Job's riches were taken away, he would abandon God. So everything is taken away, and Job is left bereft and in pain. His friends tell him to curse God and die or admit that he must have done something wrong—some ritual impurity or failure of true worship—to inspire such a level of loss and suffering. Job refuses to admit that his punishment and loss are his own fault and calls God to account, to explain this suffering. God does not explain the reason for Job's suffering, but shows that it is part of the cycle of human suffering and the ongoing course of nature.

Jung believed that this challenge to traditional ideas of reward and punishment was an extremely important development in our understanding of the divine consciousness—or as he put it, the need for God to become more conscious. In his view, this challenge to traditional ideas of reward and punishment led to the development in the collective unconscious of a need for a figure who could reunite the divine and human, thus overcoming this tension of opposites between our understanding of the divine and our experience of the nature of reality.[51]

This complex challenge to what it means to be chosen of and blessed by God is important in order for us to comprehend the tension in the meaning of the call to be the chosen people. One belief that has pervaded parts of Old Testament theology is that being chosen means God blesses your people in particular and you are destined to be a great empire, to move from being slaves in Egypt to having the right to conquer people, destroy them in the name of ethnic purity, and become a great nation. This is a theological and mythological reconstruction of the history of the "chosen people" that has little basis in historical reality. There is no evidence that even in the days of David and Solomon they were a great empire in any historical or literal sense.[52]

The other theological understanding of what it means to be the chosen people, emphasized by the prophets, is that being chosen of God means to understand the love and mercy of God and to be loving and merciful. Being chosen means to be called to be like God, this God who is a God of love and mercy who wants us to be loving and merciful. The tension between these two guiding theological images is still seen in modern Israel and Zionism, as well as in our own country. It is the tension between those who see us a "chosen people"— meaning that, in their view, we have the right to take and dominate—and those who understand that we are called to love justice and mercy, to walk humbly with our God, and to care for the poor and the unfortunate of all races and groups, not just those who are part of our country or our religion.

This belief in a loving and merciful God who demands that we also are loving and merciful is the prophetic consciousness that culminates with Jesus. The Old Testament prophets were not some magical fortunetellers who literally foresaw the coming of Jesus in great detail, but they were developers of the consciousness that he embodies and carries to its greatest development. Jesus challenged the religious leaders of his time in the same way that the prophets challenged the secular leaders of their time. It is clear now that these kings who ruled at the time of the prophets were not particularly evil or corrupt men. These kings were being challenged by the prophets to act from a higher level of consciousness, to live up to their true calling to be images of the divine rather than simply wielders of power and strategy.[53]

Theology as Emergent Understanding

I conclude this section by acknowledging that this theology of God and creation is not the one correct version of the theology of God and creation. It is in one sense my interpretation, my retelling of the story. However, it is not just my subjective creation of a story, but a reinterpretation for our time of these traditional sources of knowledge about God and creation that draws upon current scholarship and historical knowledge.

As Karen Armstrong clearly demonstrates in her scholarly examination of the roots of these scriptures titled, simply enough, The Bible,[54] there have always been reinterpretations of scripture that attempted to reformulate earlier ideas and stories to meet the needs of the time and the situation of their audience. Until recent centuries, the historical church never shared this current emphasis on recovering the literal meaning of a "divinely inspired" text. This emphasis on literal inspiration was the response of fundamentalism to the challenge of science.[55]

It appears that, historically, as science challenged many literal interpretations of the biblical accounts, some defenders of traditional religion sought to counter the emergent power of science and the enlightenment by locating the authority of these accounts in a divine, inerrant God who dictated the words to writers. This interpretation was never the understanding of the meaning of divine inspiration in the historical church, and it is not the understanding Karen Armstrong and other current biblical scholars present, neither is it my understanding.

However, this does not mean that I think that the scriptures are just ordinary human documents like any other group of stories and histories. They are inspired, and they are fundamental to our religious tradition. When understood correctly, they continue to inspire many today. In contrast to this understanding, literal fundamentalism creates a narrow and unrealistic view of a God who is only our God, and the one true God, preserved as the only correct version for all time. This literalism prevents believers from developing the ability to understand the evolving nature of the meaning of God and creation as it unfolds in light of our current understanding of reality. Our comprehension of these writings continues to evolve as the writings of the Old Testament evolved in their relationship to their time and history.

In our time, our current understanding of God cannot be separated from any knowledge or experience of reality. As science is constantly refining and developing its description of reality in the light of new knowledge, religion also is constantly evolving in the light of a new understanding of divine reality.[56]

PART TWO

JESUS AND REDEMPTION.

⚜

I N TRADITIONAL CHRISTIAN THEOLOGY, REDEMPTION IS THE second part of the divine activity (the first part being God and creation and the third being the Holy Spirit and sanctification, which I call transformation) and is connected particularly with the figure of Jesus. Historically, redemption has been the center of the Christian faith. It certainly was central as I was growing up. As a conservative Lutheran, I repeated every Sunday a confession that I was "a poor miserable sinner, sinful and unclean." I was also repeatedly told that Jesus died for my sins and the sins of the whole world, and that we were redeemed.

As a child, I never questioned the truth or the centrality of this belief. It was only later that this formulation made less and less sense to me. However, during my childhood, it was one way to create a relationship with the figure of Jesus as my ally in a world of punitive fathers and many dangers.

When I grew up and looked at this formulation of sin and redemption with more consciousness, it became clear to me that this repetition of my sinfulness—however forgiven I was—had a destructive effect on my sense of selfhood. It also postulated an arbitrary God who needed to punish someone and focused on His innocent son. Subsequently, as I became more acquainted with the words of the Gospels and the history of the movement that became known as Christianity, I came to realize that this formulation of universal sinfulness redeemed through the death of Jesus came much later in the history of Christianity and was more connected with the idea of Roman law and justice than it was with the original ideas of Christianity.[57] Recognition of this truth was a major reason I left the institutional church and looked elsewhere for my spiritual sustenance. Nevertheless, the figure of Jesus the Christ always resonated with me, and in recent years I have found it important to connect with his original mission and purpose as recorded in the Gospels.

In pursuing that connection, I have encountered the emergence of a new story about Jesus and his mission and purpose. Of course, this is not really a new story, but a return to the original story of the movement that Jesus brought to his time, which was called the Way. Jesus himself did not so much see it as a new story than as a culmination of the Old Testament prophetic tradition that he fulfilled and embodied. After his death and resurrection, no one story or theology was accepted by all his followers. Rather, differing details and emphases arose that each of the Gospels express. There were more varied stories and traditions about Jesus that continued in parallel fashion in the early years, only becoming one story at the time of Constantine and later consolidation.[58]

Because this understanding of Jesus and the Way has once again helped me find meaning and relevance in the life and person of Jesus, I am sharing the knowledge of this "new" story of Jesus. It is not new or original with me but rather based on recent historical and critical scholarship about Jesus. Many people have been sharing this awareness and this scholarship, but the great majority of people who view themselves as Christians in the United States are only recently coming to know this story as communicated by scholars such as Marcus Borg, John Dominic Crossan, Elaine Pagels, Karen Armstrong, Richard Rohr, Barbara Brown Taylor, Matthew Fox, and others.[59]

Because this "new" story has helped me in my own spiritual journey and allowed me to reconnect with Jesus and historic Christianity, and because it seems urgent for many others to understand this new story at this critical time in world and spiritual history, I am sharing some knowledge about how this mission and message of Jesus can be understood. I want to restore some of the original meanings to some of the traditional terms in this theology of Jesus and Redemption.

Redemption

The idea of redemption, while not unique to Christianity or the New Testament, has come to take on a specific meaning and theological interpretation in traditional Christianity, centering around Jesus. However, redemption has always and everywhere been part of God's activity. It is a theme in all major religions. Fall and redemption are archetypal themes throughout the Old Testament but are more clearly developed by the later prophets who frequently depict God as the lover wooing his beloved to return to him and be faithful. This message was primarily why Jesus was viewed as the culmination of the prophetic tradition. He was the divine lover manifested in earthly form, seeking to have God's people return to the Way. His mission and message were not totally new, not separate from the divine revelation that came before, but were its fulfillment.[60]

Jesus Proclaims the Presence of the Kingdom of God

One way we can understand the meaning of redemption more clearly is to look again at the original stories of Jesus and his mission. The message of Jesus, which he proclaimed from the beginning, was that the active presence of God was at work in each present moment. He announced that the kingdom of God was already here and that we needed to recognize its presence.[61] He demonstrated this divine presence by manifesting these two qualities: infinite compassion, and such a deep connection with the divine that he could experience God as *Abba*, the divine Father/Mother/Source. Out of this connection, he manifested this divine love and compassion in the form of healing the sick, welcoming the outcasts and sinners to God's gracious presence, and demonstrating a charismatic level of being that drew people to him and caused them to want to be in his presence. In other words, the original message that Jesus proclaimed was not so much one of future redemption as it was of the awareness that the redeeming presence and power of divine love is already present with us.

The Meaning of Prophecy

In the Gospels, there are various attempts to say the prophets "prophesied" the coming of Jesus. They vary and sometimes conflict in their ways of presenting this. As Karen Armstrong indicates,[62] this was a common method of reinterpreting original scriptures, and the Gospel writers did not assert that it was the original meaning. Once again, we need to move from this claim of literality to understand that the consciousness embodied in the divine message that began and developed with the writings of the prophets was seen by the Gospel writers themselves as culminating in the message and story of Jesus. That the Gospel writers linked back to the prophets was a theological statement on their part, an attempt to place Jesus as the culmination of that lineage rather than a literal or historical statement. For this reason, they did not particularly bother to harmonize the details and did not seem concerned that their accounts differed in their descriptions of these lineages.

The Old Testament and the Axial Age

The material that was later collected and revised during the Axial Age (the period of the Great Transformation, written about with great scholarship and understanding by Karen Armstrong)[63] to become what Christians have called the Old Testament was shaped by the historical situation of Israel when the oral traditions first became written documents. It was during the period of the exile that these writings were collected and formulated to speak to people who were trying to understand the meaning of their suffering. This collection of scrolls was not literally dictated by God. We say that they were divinely inspired because they were part of the emergent revelation of the history of this people's relationship with Jahweh. These writers were trying to understand the reason for their suffering and for the catastrophes that had befallen them in the form of the exile and the destruction of the temple.[64]

The Gospels Are Also Written to Struggling Believers

The Gospels were not written originally as historical accounts of events as much as sermons to the new believers in the midst of their own suffering and as records of the oral stories that had been handed down and preserved to inspire believers. Each Gospel had a particular emphasis and framework for presenting the story of Jesus and his life. While the basic framework is the same for the original three Gospels—Matthew, Mark, and Luke—each contains differing emphases and, in many instances, conflicting details.

When these collections of writings became important enough in the evolution of spiritual awareness and spoke powerfully enough to illumine the plight of people struggling with their faith, these Gospels and other stories and writings were experienced as inspired by God. Eventually, this was recognized broadly enough that they became part of the canonical, or accepted, version of scripture, i.e., the written story addressed to people to maintain their faith. This is how inspiration works. Because these Gospels spoke to people in their struggles in a creative and original way, and chronicled the figures important to these stories in a meaningful narrative that inspired the faithful, they came to be viewed as inspired.

The Purpose of the Gospels

Literal accuracy and agreement about historical details never mattered to the early t. In fact, in that era there were many more differing accounts of the message of Jesus, which continued, parallel to each other, until the time when Christianity became identified with the Roman Empire. At this time, the Emperor

Constantine wanted to establish order and unanimity so the dominant narrative could be centrally controlled.

However, there were other, more legitimate, reasons that the four canonical Gospels emerged to be the accepted—which is what canonical implies—Gospels. Alexander Shaia wrote a book about these four Gospels, entitled *Heart and Mind: The Four-Gospel Journey for Radical Transformation*,[65] which makes a great deal of sense to me and apparently to others in the progressive liturgical/biblical tradition. Shaia discovered that these four Gospels were selected not so much for their historical or "truth" factor, as for the fact that the early Church found that reading them successively provided an archetypal path for transformation. This is the reason the Gospels continued to form the liturgical framework in which the Church located its readings over a four-year cycle, until they were revised several hundred years later. This tradition of liturgical readings in this sequence was rediscovered in recent centuries and adopted by the churches that follow this liturgical tradition.[66] Their fourfold pattern provided a journey of transformation in which believers could experience themselves as part of the journey of Jesus.

The Meaning and Message of Jesus

Whether you accept Shaia's view of the liturgical role in the selection of the canonical Gospels as true or not, it seems indisputable that the message of Jesus and his earliest followers was about the immediacy of the transformative presence of the divine. He embodied this presence so completely on a personal level that he was viewed as being one with God. However, he described himself as a prototypical human, the Son of Man,[67] and invited all to share in the transformative power of that relationship. For Jesus this transformative power was not a theological belief or concept, it was a relationship. His relationship with his *Abba* created a faith (not a belief) that reached out with divine compassion and love for all beings. In some of the stories, his compassion and love reached out to the sinner and the ritually unclean to let them know they were invited to share in the Kingdom. He also reached out to heal the sick, and the healing was for all people, gentiles as well as Jews. In still other stories, he reached out to challenge the religious leaders of his day to focus on divine presence and love rather than on ritual purity or religious orthodoxy.[68]

There have always been questions about the historicity and the "accuracy" of the Gospels. One question concerns what Jesus really said, what sayings are authentically from his mouth, and what was added by the Church as the tradition developed. Thomas Jefferson, for instance, is an early Enlightenment figure who tried to sort out the true sayings of Jesus and to discover what were his authentic words.[69] While these are interesting questions of scholarship and much new material has been written about this subject, the central message of Jesus is not in question. In Matthew 25, Jesus makes it clear that the true followers of God are the ones who show compassion to the sick and imprisoned. He makes it clear that the central command required for his followers is the same as the one central to Judaism—to love God with one's entire heart, soul, and mind, and to love one's neighbor (and all are neighbors) as oneself.

However, the power behind the words that Jesus spoke came not only from what he said and taught but also from the power of divine presence that those who encountered him experienced. The Gospels are not so much an attempt to give an accurate account of the history of Jesus as an account of how he impacted and transformed people and made them more than they were. He called them to follow him, "to do even more" than he did. According to his followers' own accounts of their experiences, Jesus transformed them from simple fishermen and tradespeople to people on fire with the divine presence, people who knew that his presence was transforming the world.

Following Jesus was not an easy path, and as he went to Jerusalem following the path of destiny—as he came to understand it—his disciples were continually challenged to maintain their commitment to and faith in that destiny and presence. It demanded such a huge shift in consciousness for them that they would all fall away and scatter—except, perhaps, for John. They all went through a period of experiencing a complete sense of abandonment and despair, doubt and grieving.[70]

Again, the question of what part of this story was a singular historical event and how much of it was subsequently shaped as a teaching story told to early Christians who were going through severe challenges as Christianity spread and encountered resistance, was not relevant to the early Church. These early Christians could understand that even when their faith was tested beyond their capacity to maintain it, it was still possible for them to return and experience the resurrected presence of Jesus, as the first disciples had. They could identify with those early disciples who went from total devastation and emotional collapse to experiencing Jesus returning to them and being alive in their presence. Over time, they came to view him as becoming more than just the human, embodied Jesus. He evolved into the archetypal and triumphant Christ.[71]

I want to emphasize the point that how much of this story is literal history is being continually evaluated by biblical scholars, with various interpretations. However, for the early Church, questions of historicity and literal accuracy were beside the point. What allowed these stories to resonate and spread in the world of that time was that the lives of these followers of the Way were impacted to the extent that they came to view their experiences as having cosmic significance. The impact of these experiences of the presence and power of Jesus led to heartfelt convictions that were powerful enough to move them to leave their ordinary lives and want to share the Way with everyone.

One question that scholars debate currently: did Jesus really predict his death and resurrection, or was that a reconstruction that early followers projected back after they had gone through the whole experience? Perhaps it was both— the awareness on the part of Jesus that this was a destiny he needed to follow to its end; and the reconstruction of his death and resurrection as a fulfillment of prophecy by the disciples as they came to experience his presence with them after his death. This kind of reconstruction of a story as divinely predicted was a common practice.[72]

Another reason the Way spread so rapidly and impacted the world was that these early Christians, the followers of the Way, lived their message. They shared with one another, and especially with those in need. They created systems of administration that allowed all to share in the benevolence, and for many in that world this was a powerful testimony and appeal. This aspect of sharing is detailed in the Book of Acts, which records some of that early history and contains those words that seem so significant but are so often glossed over: they "shared all things in common."[73]

As I have outlined earlier, according to Old Testament scholarship (especially as presented by Karen Armstrong, but based on the work of many scholars), Old Testament writers and compilers took stories and framed them in terms that could speak to the devastation of the exiles. In the same manner, the early Christians took the oral stories and written sources (there was an early document that recorded many of the early stories about and quotations from Jesus)[74] and framed them in a story written to respond to the situation of the current disciples. The earliest written account, that of the Gospel of Mark, which Karen Armstrong and the majority of current scholars date to around 70 CE, was not produced until around forty years after the death of Jesus.[75]

In subsequent years, many versions of this Gospel story emerged that were centered around particular figures in the early Church. Since the discovery of the many apocryphal gospels (apocryphal in this context meaning gospels that were accepted by various Christian communities in the centuries before the Council of Nicaea but were not accepted as canonical at that time), we know that different communities in the early Church created stories that differed in emphasis and detail according to the meaning developed within that community. There were gospels attributed to Thomas, to Phillip, and to Mary the Magdalenian, among others. These are some of the most well known that have been preserved, but there were many other versions.[76]

Also, in the early years of this movement known as the Way, these new followers did not view themselves as a new and separate religion but as a pure and culminating form of Judaism, a reform movement within Judaism. Jesus's brother James was the dominant figure among these early followers, and the movement centered in Jerusalem.[77] However, from the beginning the movement was centered on Jesus and on the transformative impact he made in their lives. These first followers of the Way shared the story of how he had come as the great healer, prophet, and reformer to proclaim the active presence of God in the world. They had gone through a devastating experience of loss, denial, and disappointment when he was crucified but had experienced him as returning to them again in visible and tangible form. This central story of death and rebirth, or death and resurrection, has an archetypal resonance that still speaks to us today as Christians again experience devastating loss or see the tragic ways in which the powerful dominate and crucify those who oppose them. True followers often go through these times of doubt and despair yet today.

The Early Community After the Time of Jesus

Two movements developed over time among these early followers of the Way. As the movement continued to spread, a tension developed between the followers of James, who continued to follow the central practices and rituals of Judaism, and those who came to believe they were called to transcend the traditions of Judaism, that the ritual laws of Judaism no longer needed to be followed. Paul of Tarsus, whom we have come to know as the Apostle Paul, became the leader and advocate for this second movement to separate the new religion of the Way from the rituals and requirements of the Jewish religion of his time.[78]

This split among the early followers eventuated in the branch following Paul becoming dominant, especially as it moved into the Graeco-Roman world, which was the focus of Paul. It finally culminated in a split between Judaism and Christianity. It is hard to know with certainty exactly how and when the division between Judaism and the early followers of the Way developed. Certainly, Jesus was crucified by the political powers of his time. However, the earlier accounts portray it as more of a Roman response to another reformer who might be a threat and challenge to their control rather than as a Jewish conspiracy.[79]

It was true that some of the religious leaders who operated in Jerusalem at that time were collaborators with the Roman powers, but they were, like Herod and his sons, leaders who were permitted to operate by the Roman government on the condition that they collaborated. For them as well, Jesus may have been viewed as a threat to the coexistence that had been attained between religious and Roman authorities. However, he was viewed by these religious leaders as more of a threat to institutional and political religious structures than as a challenge to the religion itself. Jesus, in his own words, made it clear that he was a true follower of the Torah, the basic foundational writings of Judaism.[80]

There appears to have been a connection between Jesus's challenge to the pervasive corruption of the temple—his cleansing of the temple of the merchants who were fleecing the people who came to worship—and his crucifixion. In any case, his confrontations with these authorities were never presented in the first three Gospels as a challenge to Jewish religion. Rather, they were framed as a cleansing and challenging of religious and institutional structures that were more about self-preservation and personal purity than about loving God with all one's heart and soul and mind and loving one's neighbor as oneself. This was a tension that existed within Judaism itself. To summarize: for the earliest followers, Jesus was the embodiment and culmination of the Jewish faith.

One puzzling aspect of subsequent history is how the Pharisees came to be delineated as the evil opponents of Jesus. This delineation is not so characteristic of the earliest Gospel, Mark, in which at the beginning of Jesus's ministry, John the Baptizer's call to repentance is directed at everyone in his audience. However, in the Gospel of Matthew, which was written later, this call to repentance is presented as a direct and specific challenge to the Sadducees and Pharisees.[81] The

Pharisees were, in fact, a relatively progressive group, and much of their later teaching, which culminated in the rabbinic tradition, would have been similar to the teachings that Jesus shared. Several of the early followers of Jesus were Pharisees, and the prominent teacher Gamaliel is recorded as advising religious leaders of that time to avoid persecuting these early followers of Jesus.[82]

The apostle Paul, as indicated earlier, was instrumental in separating this new faith from its Jewish roots. He did this, at least in part, to make the Way more universal; to appeal to the non-Jewish population of the Graeco-Roman world of his day. He believed that he had been given this specific mission by Jesus during his vision on the road to Damascus.[83] If there was a personal element to this mission, it may be that Paul, as all people who go through a significant conversion experience, shifted from being a zealous Pharisee to one who wanted to completely separate from that tradition. Over time, his version of the Way came to be the one that dominated in the early Church and moved it from a reformist movement within Judaism to a more universal faith centered on the figure of Jesus as the Christ.[84]

Two historical events also contributed to the split. One was the persecution of the Jewish community under Nero in Rome. Nero was looking for a scapegoat to deflect the anger of the Roman people that was directed toward him for his profligacy and mismanagement. He found it in the Jewish community at the edge of Rome, which contained both the followers of Jesus and traditional synagogue Jews. As the persecution gradually shifted its focus to the early Christians, the synagogue community may have distanced themselves from the early Christians (and/or vice versa). This is the locus of the Gospel of Mark, which was written for Christians going through severe trials to their faith under this persecution.[85]

The second major event that occasioned the split was the complete destruction of the temple in Jerusalem in 70 CE. This total destruction of Jerusalem and the temple by the Romans effectively ended the role of the temple and the system of sacrifices that had played such a central role in previous forms of Judaism. This seems to be the occasion for the Gospel of Matthew.[86] For both the early followers of the Way and the Jewish believers, this was a devastating event that challenged their faith in a God who could allow this to happen. As a result of the destruction of this central religious focus, the Pharisees and rabbinic Judaism came to play a more prominent role in the Jewish community at large and developed Judaism as a more universal religion with a following throughout the early diaspora—the dispersed Jewish people who were settling in various parts of the Graeco-Roman world. Some of the early Christians began to view rabbinic Judaism as the primary competing religious movement in that early world.[87]

A subsequent development that precipitated the separation between Jews and early Christians was that over time, the figure of Jesus had come to be more universally viewed as the Christ, the Messiah, by many of his followers, especially in the Graeco-Roman world. For his first disciples, their early experiences of shock and disappointment after the crucifixion had been transformed into joy and faith as they were told that Jesus was still alive and present with them. Later tradition collapsed this into a resurrection that occurred after three days to give it more symbolic meaning. However, the first Gospel, Mark, in its original ending simply tells the story of a young man dressed in white who tells the women who come to the tomb to tell the disciples to go and meet Jesus in Galilee. They are still so much in shock that they do not tell anyone. There was no physical reappearance recorded in Mark. This ending was so difficult for later Christians that they added a less troubling ending.[88]

Regardless of how the resurrection event was mythologized or condensed to fit a narrative later, what we do know is that these early followers experienced Jesus's presence and aliveness with them in a transformed state. He was no longer confined to a human body but would be with them wherever they were. He "poured down his Spirit" upon them, inspiring them with new faith, courage, and knowledge. The physical, human Jesus of history was, over time, transformed into the Christ of faith.[89]

In pointing out this historical fact, I do not mean to

denigrate or challenge this development. As Richard Rohr, Marcus Borg, and other contemporary progressive writers have indicated, the idea of the Logos (the original pattern behind the universe that is manifested in Jesus) and the idea of the Christ (the Anointed One, or the Messiah) also predate the historical Jesus and contain larger collective patterns of expectation.[90] In Christianity, these patterns came to be viewed as manifested in Jesus, the Logos, the Christ. This development was part of the natural evolution that also emerged around other central religious figures, such as the Buddha or Mohammed. These pivotal beings had such a profound impact that they were experienced as transcending and changing the reality of their time. The followers of the Way eventually evolved into the religion of the early Christians who believed that Jesus was the true Messiah. We can see the evolution of this idea emerging in the writings of Paul. As heW emphasized in telling his story, Paul never met the human, historical Jesus "in the flesh."[91] His powerful encounter with Jesus was a mystical appearance that occurred in a blinding, overwhelming vision on the road to Damascus. Because his only experience of Jesus was as the risen, transcendent Christ, Jesus became for Paul the one who manifested divine nature in human form, who provides a link between ordinary humans and the divinity.

For Paul, this understanding of Jesus was not theoretical or intellectual. His mystical encounter with the transcendent Jesus on the road to Damascus was an experience that affected him so powerfully that it permanently transformed his life and gave it a new direction and purpose.[92] As a result of this experience of participation in the divine nature, Paul taught that all humans could so completely identify with this figure of Jesus as the Christ that they, too, could participate in the transcendent divine nature.[93]

For him, and for other earliest followers of the Way, there was no developed theory of redemption, such as the Atonement Theory—the theory, developed over time, that Jesus took our place and died to atone for our sins. Rather they believed that the death and resurrection of Jesus was a transformative event that had changed their lives and could change the lives of the people to whom they reached out to share this good news. They also believed that this event signaled the fulfillment of Old Testament and Messianic expectations. They developed differing versions of this story about the life and ministry of Jesus to appeal to their specific audiences. For example, the way the story was framed was different for Jewish Christian audiences than for Graeco-Roman gentile audiences.[94]

The Meaning of Jesus for Later Generations

Subsequent generations of followers would develop their own language for describing the meaning of the life and mission of Jesus, and the particularity of that meaning again varied with differing cultures and traditions. For instance, the Eastern (Orthodox) Catholic Church "portrays redemption in positive terms whereby one is called to really participate in the personal and divine energies of the Trinity as a result of the Incarnation of Jesus Christ." In the Western (Roman) Catholic Church, it was formulated in more legal terms, as a substitutionary atonement, meaning that Jesus is the substitute sacrifice to atone for our sins.[95]

For current Evangelical Protestant theology, these two historical, more flexible interpretations have been frozen into a more narrow, dogmatized theology. For them, there is only one correct way of understanding the meaning of redemption. The basic elements of this way of understanding redemption are: the recognition of human separation or sinfulness; the belief that this separation has been overcome through Jesus; and the conviction that we can begin a new life in Christ through the power of the Holy Spirit.

This basic story is still a potent transformative and redemptive story for many people. There are many even today who have experienced themselves as freed from separation and bondage by the death of Jesus for their sins, which gives them the freedom of a new life. This belief often has had transformative power, especially for people who have experienced themselves as caught in addictions or compulsions.[96]

Unfortunately, many traditional Christians have turned

this belief into a rigid formula, including the requirement of believing that this is the only redemptive story. This rigidity of belief, in turn, leads these "true believers" to a need to convert, to see others as less than, and to project their shadow onto others who do not share their formula. This is a belief in salvation by formula, not by faith.

Nevertheless, other contemporary Christians, such as Annie Lamott and Rob Bell, really live and understand this theology in a way that allows them, like Paul, to experience an overwhelming sense of the grace that transforms them, that allows them to live in Christ.[97]

Other Redemption Stories

The redemption story summarized above is not the only way of understanding redemption today, even among Christians. Other stories of redemption are found in other religions of the world, and redemptive experiences occur outside of a religious framework as well. For instance, many people described in the literature about entheogenic experiences (entheogenic is a term literally meaning "creating the divine within," referring to mind-altering substances) have experienced a new unity with the divine and a freedom from old patterns of seeing and experiencing the world mediated by these substances. I have known some of these people personally. To cite one example, the Swiss chemist Albert Hofmann, the discoverer of LSD, had his own powerful spiritual trips.[98]

It is also true that these powerful substances need to be used with care and preparation. For some people, the experiences arising from ingesting these substances have been destructive, especially when taken in the wrong dosage and setting. Many societies have used entheogens in their religious and spiritual rites but usually within the framework of a group culture and belief system and guided by a leader who helped them through the initiatory and transformative process.

However, this redemption story is not about entheogens; it is about the fact that there have always been and still are many differing stories and experiences of redemption today.

Many traditional Christians experience this expanded idea of redemption as an affront or a challenge to their belief that there is only one way of redemption. However, this broader understanding of redemption was historically present in the early Church.[99] Even John Calvin, one of the leading figures of the Reformation, believed that the great spiritual giants of classical time, such as Plato and Socrates, would also be found in heaven.[100] Pope John XXIII in 1962 issued an official statement, called *Nostra Aetate*, that recognized the truth in all religions.[101]

To use an analogy, we know that in the universe there are many suns and many solar systems. This discovery does not lessen the value of the sun for us on Earth, even though many people at the time of this discovery of other suns thought this fact was a threat to their personal and religious beliefs.[102] In the same way, the awareness that there are other powerful central figures and other redemptive experiences does not lessen the value of the one we have called the Son.

I want to offer another example of a redemptive story from my personal experience. I was privileged to be present for a Lakota Sun Dance, a powerful and transformative ritual for the participants and observers. I was able to take part in this religious ceremony for several years. It has several of the same elements as the Christian redemption story. For example, the dancers view their suffering as something that is done for the sake of others, as suffering that is transformative and redemptive. Many broken lives, caught in the wake of the group trauma of the physical and cultural destruction of their ancestors, were healed through this ritual. It was a powerful way of healing trauma and finding a meaning powerful enough to free many dancers from patterns that had been destructive in their lives.

One of the tragedies of our own nation's religious history is that, instead of building on that commonality with indigenous beliefs and sharing the insights of Christianity while learning from the original inhabitants about their own powerful insights, we tried to exterminate their religions even as we literally destroyed them. This destruction was often sanctioned by religious leaders.[103] (The novel *Sacred Wilderness* by Susan

Powers brings these differences and similarities into a modern setting, demonstrating brilliantly what we could learn from their way of experiencing this redemption story.)[104]

For many of us today, however, the traditional version of the Christian redemption story is no longer effective because we no longer experience ourselves as "sinners in the hands of an angry God."[105] However, there are many people today who do experience themselves rather as lost people who are separated from any sense of connection with the divine, from connection with one another, and from a sense of meaning or purpose in life.

We often experience ourselves as part of a world that is increasingly polarized into rich and poor, developed and undeveloped. Many of us have felt powerless, caught in overwhelming systems that appear to be leading to our destruction and the destruction of the world as we know it today. We not only need traditional individual salvation, we need the redemption of a culture that is careening headlong toward its own destruction. It is important to point out that these are not mutually exclusive, but synergistic. A genuine individual transformation leads to compassion and care for other people and the world, and the transformation of all facilitates the transformation of the individual.

What Is the Redemption Story That Can Speak to This Crisis?

For many of our contemporaries, the redemptive process is not viewed as arising from a belief or a set of beliefs but from a set of practices. Many religious, spiritual, and non-religious people are finding personal healing through meditation practices or through yoga and breathwork practices. One reason meditation practices have become central to many is that they do not require a belief but rather a consistent set of practices. Many practitioners find that they discover a sense of inner peace, acceptance, trust, and freedom from compulsive behaviors. Mindfulness, a central practice for many meditators, is now an important component in much current psychotherapy and other forms of holistic healing.

This practice has helped many to redeem their lives from anxiety and meaninglessness.[106]

Others today find that their lives are redeemed through participating in work to transform their society, whether it is directed toward a passion for justice, a concern for all sentient creatures, or efforts to change destructive lifestyles into sustainable lifestyles. There are also people who are motivated not by any religious vision or orientation, but by love and compassion and a new vision of possibilities for humanity. Three examples from many I could name are Jane Goodall, Greta Thunberg, and Charles Eisenstein.

A Tragic View of Redemption

Before moving on to look at possible redemptive stories for today, I would like to outline one false, misleading, and destructive idea of redemption that has persisted among a significant element of the Judeo-Christian tradition. This false notion of the meaning of redemption and the purpose of the Messiah is the belief in a Messiah who will be a dominating conqueror, who will destroy the enemies and wreak vengeance on oppressors.[107] This is a strain of belief that grew out of the dominator theology that runs throughout elements of the Old Testament and continues today.[108] This belief that the Messiah would set the world aright was developed to give meaning to suffering, a meaning that appealed often to those who saw themselves as the "chosen" people. They did not understand why, if they were the chosen people, and if they followed the true God who chose them, they were subject to such catastrophes as exile and captivity. I alluded to this earlier in the section on the meaning of Old Testament themes. This was the locus of their belief that a Suffering Servant would come to restore the (mythologized) greatness of Israel. This belief maintained that if they were righteous and pure enough, God would save and justify them by placing them in a dominant position over other nations.

This response to catastrophe and helplessness often took the form of a reformist zeal that, for instance, under King Josiah, led to the destruction and exile of many in his kingdom. His actions only alienated his country from the dominant empire of his time and led to severe reprisals.[109]

This sense of helplessness and oppression led to the development of a compensatory belief that a great king and Messiah would come to restore a power and greatness that never actually existed and led to an expectation that would never be fulfilled in history, no matter how pure or fanatical they were. Throughout biblical history, this zeal for "true belief" led to the kind of destruction the Romans inflicted on Jerusalem.[110]

We can admire the courage and commitment of some of these purist reformers, but the results of these reforms and their failure to be in touch with political reality led to terrible suffering and destruction for many around them as well as for themselves.

This was the messianic expectation that Jesus encountered throughout his ministry, even among his disciples. Even when he clearly spelled out his purpose and mission to them, they were still so caught up in their expectation that Jesus would somehow fulfill their Messianic expectations that his failure to fight, to respond to the power of the Roman empire with greater legions of his own, led to their melting away during his captivity and execution—except, as previously noted, perhaps for John.[111]

Even after his death and transcendence, many of his followers still believed that Jesus would return in a cloud of glory at any moment and ultimately establish his rule on earth. As this longed-for event failed to materialize, this expectation was moved to a vision that at some point in the future end times, the righteous would be living in endless bliss in a place they called heaven, and the wicked would be punished in hell. This expectation developed because of the strong need among "true believers" to believe that there would be an ultimate vindication of their beliefs. However, Jesus never taught that the world would at some future date be reshaped by a messianic figure. Instead, he proclaimed that the presence of God in the world was transforming it. His followers were not chosen to be part of a restoration of temporal power, they were chosen to carry his message of the redeeming and loving presence of God in the world.[112]

When the end times did not happen and when persecution and suffering again became acute, this vision of the ultimate validation of "true believers" re-emerged in the book of Revelation. It evolved into an expectation of an ultimate battle between good and evil, in which the dominator version of Jesus would come and defeat the forces of evil forever. Ever since this original apocalyptic vision, which developed around the end of the first century,[113] bands of "true believers" and people suffering under oppression have been certain that the signs and portents were in their time portending the fulfillment of the prophecy that good would finally win over evil and the proper order of the world would be restored. None of these expectations has support in the words and actions of Jesus, and there is no biblical support for the idea of a Rapture. These apocalyptic visions derive from the powerful need of some people to be vindicated in a tangible and immediate way for their beliefs and the need of others to believe in some future idealized time and space that would deliver them from their present suffering.

Because many people who hold these beliefs hold positions of power in our government as well as the reality that messianic beliefs have a strong constituency in the nation of Israel, these beliefs in the evil and suffering of this world which will be compensated by some future state of vindication again threaten to bring about great destruction. These "true believers" tend to become more estranged from reality as they become more desperate to see their apocalyptic visions fulfilled. Another current example of this need for vindication is the senators and congressmen who deny climate change because of a conviction that God will intervene to save us if we just trust enough in their unique vision. Since this world is soon disappearing, we have a right and a command to dominate and use up natural resources. When reality does not conform to these expectations, they tend to become even more confirmed in their illusory convictions. This pattern has been amply documented by research.[114]

In reaction to this phenomenon, there are many intelligent

people in this country, in Israel, and in the developed world who think that this irrational apocalyptic belief proves that there is a deep chasm between religion and science/reality, and therefore, they want nothing to do with religion.

Meaningful Stories of Redemption for Our Time

In contrast to that apocalyptic vision, many people today have a totally different vision of the need for and meaning of redemption. Their understanding is that God is at work in this present world through all of us, and it is our task to share in this work of moving toward peace and unification here and now rather than awaiting some divine rescue.

This version of the redemption story emerged out of the prophetic tradition and culminates in the message of Jesus that can provide meaning and transformation for our time. It is a story about the divine presence in our world that allows us to understand and participate in the transformation of consciousness that must occur if we are to survive without a period of incredible trauma and destruction. We cannot force the hand of some great father God to save us by bringing about the destruction of the earth on which we live; we can only participate in the change of consciousness that is required if this earth is to survive. The alternative is for our choices to be more and more isolated from reality. We can be children pouting because God does not save us from our folly and put us in charge of the world, or mature Christians who participate in the co-creation and co-evolution of this world that has been given to us. We can shrink the definitions of Christian and of God, or we can expand them to see the divine presence at work in our world today, calling us to participate in the Great Transformation that is possible with the development of more consciousness.

Teilhard de Chardin, one of the great scientists and religions visionaries of the twentieth century, is a pioneer in articulating this evolutionary vision for our time. He was a Jesuit and a prominent scientist who in his time won great recognition for his significant work in paleontology. At the same time he was a great mystic who, through a series of mystical visions, was able to see the divine presence and energy everywhere in the world but especially in and through the physical world and nature. As a result of his mystical experiences, he came to understand that all matter is sacred, and our physical/material world is in the process of evolution and transformation.[115]

After these visionary insights, Chardin saw the need for science and religion to undergo a transformation that would lead them to understand that they are complementary ways to understand divine presence in the world rather than antagonists. He viewed the process of evolution as the unfolding of that divine presence and as a continuing incarnation of the Christ. His redemptive story is the vision of Christ continuing to incarnate as the divine unfolding of love and purpose in and through matter. In contrast to a theory of atonement, this is a vision of at-one-ment that grew out of his vision of the unity of all being. Chardin's vision is not focused on original sin, but rather on original and ongoing blessing. A life in this material world is not a curse but a blessing. For Chardin, Christ embodies the Omega point, the point toward which evolution is moving us.[116]

Chardin's work has been developed by people who shared and expanded his vision, such as Thomas Berry, Brian Swimme, and Ilia Delio.[117] Many others have been inspired in their work and life by this prophetic vision.

Another important recent prophetic voice is that of Leo Tolstoi, the great Russian writer, who lived and wrote his redemptive vision. He took seriously the words of Jesus about being a radical embodiment of divine presence in the world. He considered this work more important than the great writing he had done and devoted the last part of his life to following this call to live the life of Jesus.[118] It was, in turn, his life and writings that inspired Gandhi in his powerful life and message of nonviolence. Subsequently, they were the inspiration for Martin Luther King, Jr. All three of these men believed that the redemption story was expressed most powerfully in our passion for justice and in lives of integrity and compassion. Their vision of redemption became a very powerful force and continues to be transformative in our time. Others, such as Nelson Mandela and Desmond Tutu have been inspired in turn. Many today who do not consider themselves Christian or may identify with another religion have been inspired and transformed by this vision of non-violent transformation.

My Preferred Redemption Story for Today

My choice for the most important prophetic voice of our time is Pope Francis. In his life and his words, he tells a redemptive story that can give meaning and transformation to our presently beleaguered planet. Like St. Paul, Hildegarde of Bingen, St. Francis, Chardin and many others, he is not operating out of a belief system so much as a personal mystical experience that transformed his life into a genuine endeavor to live the life that Paul described as taking on the mind of Christ.[119] His vision has elements of all of these figures—the grace and love that Paul experienced, the courage and vision that allowed Hildegarde to confront institutional injustices, the extension of this vision to all creatures and to the whole earth that Francis experienced, and Chardin's sense of a cosmic purpose at work to integrate even the physical and political world.

Pope Francis clearly and articulately expressed this vision in two accessible places. The first of these is the encyclical *Laudato Si': On Care for Our Common Home*.[120] This encyclical translates the Christ vision into a powerful, timely, and transformative call to, in the words of Bill McKibben in the *New York Review of Books*, "change how we inhabit this planet—an ecological critique, yes, but also a moral, social, economic, and spiritual commentary."[121] The second is his address to the United States Congress in 2015. Every word of that address is a summons to live a transformative, redemptive vision of the challenge and possibility of religion in the world today. I could quote every word of that speech as an articulate expression of the redemptive story for today. In the encyclical and address, as well as his whole body of words and actions, Pope Francis has made religion—and Christianity—relevant again in the world. He has directly challenged that dominator theology that has been so pervasive in his own church and in the leadership of the United States Congress.

In his own words,

All of us are quite aware of, and deeply worried by, the disturbing social and political situation of the world today. Our world is increasingly a place of violent conflict, hatred, and brutal atrocities, committed even in the name of God and of religion. We know that no religion is immune from forms of individual delusion or ideological extremism. This means that we must be especially attentive to every type of fundamentalism, whether religious or of any other kind. A delicate balance is required to combat violence perpetuated in the name of a religion, an ideology or an economic system, while also safeguarding religious freedom, intellectual freedom, and individual freedoms. But there is another temptation which we must especially guard against: the simplistic reductionism which sees only good or evil; or, if you will, the righteous and sinners. The contemporary world, with its open wounds which affect so many of our brothers and sisters, demands that we confront every form of polarization which would divide it into these two camps. We know that in the attempt to be freed of the enemy without, we can be tempted to feed the enemy within. To imitate the hatred and violence of tyrants and murderers is the best way to take their place. That is something which you, as a people, reject.

Our response must instead be one of hope and healing, of peace and justice. We are asked to summon the courage and the intelligence to resolve today's many geopolitical and economic crises. Even in the developed world, the effects of unjust structures and actions are all too apparent. Our efforts must aim at restoring hope, righting wrongs, maintaining commitments, and thus promoting the well-being of individuals and peoples. We must move forward together, as one, in a renewed spirit of fraternity and solidarity, cooperating generously for the common good.[122]

PART THREE

THE HOLY SPIRIT
AND TRANSFORMATION

❦

FOR MANY WHO SEE THEMSELVES AS CHRISTIANS TODAY, the term Holy Spirit remains either abstract or irrelevant, out of place in the modern world. In fact, for most contemporary people, the idea of a Trinity within the divine nature also seems abstract and irrelevant.

I understand this response because it characterized my own reaction to these concepts for many years. As I grew up, the Holy Spirit was often related to the past, the source of inspiration for biblical writers, or was associated with a kind of emotional zeal, often experienced during adolescence. Then it became irrelevant, as did most of Christian theology. It seemed one of those ideas that people had passionately fought about and argued about but was as out-of-date as the idea of a tripartite universe, the three-layered view of the universe underlying the cosmology of that time.[123]

More recently, as I returned to looking at the more integral meaning of traditional Christian theology, the ideas of Trinity and Holy Spirit again began to have meaning. The idea that we can know the essence and nature of ultimate reality or that we can capture it in a permanent, fixed form makes no more sense than the idea that we can understand and capture the nature of physical reality in any ultimate, fixed form. God/reality is not a static, permanent thing. We understand "in part,"[124] and we constantly change our understanding in the light of new knowledge. It is clear from our study of nature and the universe that everything is continuously evolving; likewise, our understanding of nature and the universe is continuously evolving. The more we know, the more mysterious and complex is our understanding of any aspect of reality.

Parallel to our general understanding of reality, our conception of God has continued to evolve and become more integrative and complex. The more we know, the more difficulty we have in describing this reality in any permanent or essential form. The mystics in all religions who have had a direct encounter with the divine, who have experienced some form of oneness with the transcendent are the ones who best know the impossibility of capturing this reality in words or in any permanent form. They also understand that the essence of this reality is relational, and that the essential element of their experience of the divine is relational. For them, this divine/human relationship is also active, a movement into and through their lives in a transformational matrix.

A Contemporary Formulation of Trinity and Holy Spirit

In the same way, the concept of the Trinity is not some ultimate description of a permanent reality somewhere beyond and above and outside of us. It is, rather, a description of how those in the Christian tradition have come to understand and describe the unfolding nature of the divine. We have come to understand this nature through biblical revelation and, for Christians, its completion in the form of Jesus, who in the Christian tradition expresses in his life the reality of the divine nature. But we also know the nature of the divine—as much, that is, as we can ever know something that is beyond grasping at any moment in time or space—through understanding the world and physical reality.

We know that in some fundamental way, matter, energy, and gravity are elemental forces that underlie all physical reality. It is their interaction, their relationship, that forms and moves the universe. These concepts are ways of describing reality as we know it and measure it. They are not entities, but active forces that compose and move the universe. This understanding gives us a better sense of what is meant by the Trinity as a process underlying the basic interactive nature of the divine.

Holy Spirit and Transformation

In traditional Christian theology, the Holy Spirit is the third aspect of the ongoing process of creation/redemption/ transformation, the aspect that has been traditionally called "sanctification." In the churches that follow a liturgical calendar, this process of sanctification, or the Christian life, relates to the third part of the liturgical year, which begins with the celebration of Pentecost. This festival commemorates the occasion of the outpouring of the Holy Spirit on that early group of followers of the Way, an outpouring that brought unity and transformation to that group, transcending the barriers of language and culture. This event also began the transformation of the movement from a small group of huddled, shocked, uncertain followers of Jeshua who were recovering from the physical loss of their leader into a group that impacted the world around them.[125]

Therefore, I prefer talking about ongoing transformation rather than sanctification. The word sanctification has a quality that is expressed in the words "sanctity" and "sanctimonious." It seems to convey the sense of an individual becoming holier rather than the active presence of God transforming the world through the energy of the Holy Spirit. When understood in its true, holistic sense, holiness is a quality to be valued, but unfortunately, it is usually understood in a moral sense rather than as the awareness of the sacred in all things. This awareness of the sacred seems to convey more of the significance of the words of Paul: "Do not conform to the pattern of this world, but be transformed by the renewing of your mind."[126] (Romans 12:2, NIV) These earlier followers of the Way were not sanctimonious or even necessarily models of moral probity. They were simply human beings who were on fire with the energy and passion ignited by this outpouring of the active and present Spirit of Christ that accompanied them as they went about their mission in the world. The infusion of this present and active Spirit was manifested in a spirit of passion and commitment, but even more by the marks of love, joy, and peace.

Holy Spirit as Interactive Process

When we talk about the Holy Spirit, we are not talking about some separate being or entity. We are talking about an interactive process of the divinity as humans have come to understand it in this tradition, and all three aspects are eternally present. Creation did not end with the accounts of creation in Genesis but is manifested in a continuing evolution of life. Incarnation did not end when Jesus physically left the world, but the divine presence is continuing to incarnate in our world today and is manifested in other religious traditions as well. The work of the Holy Spirit did not begin with events of the New Testament, but that active power and presence of divine Spirit in the world has been manifesting as the expression of that divine life and energy from the beginning of existence. In those earliest creation accounts, the Spirit is present at creation, as indicated by the fact that the *Ruach*, or spirit/breath of God, "moved upon the face of the waters,"[127] (Genesis 1:2, ASV) i.e., was the active power in creation. One traditional term for the Holy Spirit is the *Spiritus Creator*, the creative spirit, which is present in every act of creation and is the active principle of the divine manifested in evolution.

This Spirit, or active energy presence of the divine, was also present in the process of incarnation and redemption, announcing the coming presence to Mary and descending in the form of a dove at the baptism of Jesus.[128]

At the risk of appearing repetitive for some readers, I want to reiterate the understanding that the stories of the descent of the dove at the baptism of Jesus and descending in tongues of fire may well be a re-creation and condensation in mythological and symbolic form of a process that occurred over time, but it is nevertheless a description of something that happened in the life of Jesus and the early life of the followers of the Way. This interpretation is not an attempt to evaluate truth or untruth in some contemporary, rational sense, but rather an attempt to convey the way stories of significant events were told in the New Testament as they were passed down over time—to convey the significance within that community of those singular events.

The Gifts of the Spirit

In the letters of Paul, the Holy Spirit is the active presence of Jesus, now transformed into the Christ, the transcendent One. It is that Spirit who bestows the gifts that Paul experienced as a result of the transformation that happened to him when he was caught up in his vision of the Christ on the road to Damascus. In this view, the spirit of Jesus continued to live in and through his followers as the divine power and presence of love and reconciliation in the world. For Paul, it was the Holy Spirit that allowed him that vision of Jesus.[129]

At the time of the writings attributed to or associated with John, the beloved disciple, the early Christians were beginning to experience persecution and suffering. In the Gospel of John, the early Christians needed comfort, an advocate to help them know that God was present with them even in their suffering. In that Gospel, Jesus in his final discourse promises that he will send them an advocate, a comforter, which is another term for the Holy Spirit.[130] It is this active presence of Spirit that would come to help them understand that their suffering was not a mark of failure or disfavor, but was due to the oppression of this new movement by the entrenched powers, primarily the Roman Empire.[131]

The Meaning and Essence of the Term Holy

It may be natural at this point to ask why this active divine energy came to be called the Holy Spirit. I do not know the historical reason for this terminology, but my personal understanding of this term is that when we are filled with the

Holy Spirit, we are filled with the numinous experience of Sacred Presence. When we are filled with that presence, we see all of life and the natural world as alive with that presence, as Chardin, Blake, and Rumi did. Chardin believed that the divine presence was incarnating in the world continually as a manifestation of the presence of the Christ in our physical, material world. This vision allowed him to see the presence of Christ throughout the physical world around him in China, and out of this vision he celebrated the Mass of the World.[132] In Chardin's Spirit-filled vision, this presence/aliveness/sense of purpose manifested in the Christ was now present not only in the sanctified bread and wine of the Mass but in all of matter and nature. When we are open to seeing that divine presence, all matter becomes numinous.

This spirit manifestation is also called Holy because it is transcendent, not limited by human structures or forms. Like the wind, which "blows where it wills"[133] and brings balance to nature, so the Holy Spirit creates and activates balance and wholeness wherever people are open to this divine presence and aliveness (and sometimes even where they are not).

When we are filled with the Holy Spirit, we become an expression of the divine presence in our world. That presence is one of love, creativity, and purpose. It is the energetic movement toward integration and wholeness. The word "Holy" in this context connotes the presence of the Sacred; but, in Chardin's vision, it is more actively the presence of evolutionary purpose moving toward an ultimate wholeness and integration that he called the Omega Point.[134]

This presence of purpose and integration is also manifested through inspiration. The Holy Spirit inspires through communication—individually, as people are open to communication and, more collectively, as particular groups are inspired with new visions or insights. This inspiration certainly came in the form of sacred and inspired writings in the past but is equally present now. It is not limited to books or churches or religions, or to the past. Barbara Brown Taylor, an Episcopal priest and popular writer, writes eloquently of this freedom and transcendence of the Spirit today. She has shared her experience of learning to see the presence of this Spirit outside of the Church. Examples she gives are any creative or original artistic creation that moves people to an original vision or a new integrative understanding of material reality.[135]

The Holy Spirit is also Holy because it transcends any religion, ideology, politics, or writings. For Christians, the Holy Spirit has always been closely associated with Jesus and has been viewed as a gift arising out of the connection with Jesus the Christ. This energy essence may not be called the Holy Spirit in other traditions, but the same essential experience is described in other religions. In the Lakota way, it is named the *Wakan Tanka*, the Great Spirit. In many traditions of the East, the active, energetic divine energy is called *chi* or *prana*. In Thich Nhat Han's introduction to Thomas Merton's book on contemplative prayer, he refers several times to the Holy Spirit.[136] Obviously, he may be using this term because it is familiar to Merton's readers, but he clearly understands the experience underlying the meaning of this term (the theological meaning is not so important). What is important is that people from many traditions and parts of the world have tuned into this active presence of divine energy, this Holy Spirit.

We now know from Einstein and his successors that this universe and the matter that comprises our own corner of it are not inert, but that there is a constant flow of energy interacting with matter. This reality has been intuited by indigenous people throughout history. Those who live in nature often continue to maintain this awareness, which most of us lose as we become socialized in the urban cultures of today. It is this energetic aspect of divine presence that has been experienced in the form of spirits (or energetic presences) in the world that Christians experience as the Holy Spirit. It is this Holy Spirit that Christians have viewed as actively and energetically present in the world through the presence of the Christ, the Logos, and Sophia (three terms used for this incarnational presence). This relationship with Jesus is the source that activates and empowers the transformative presence of the divine energy moving toward transcendence and unification for all of creation.

However, a new understanding of the activity of the Holy Spirit is necessary today to allow religion to remain relevant and enable humanity to survive. It is this new understanding of the Holy Spirit that is articulated by Pope Francis and the Dalai Lama, but is more completely articulated in the vision and the work of Teilhard de Chardin.[137]

At this point, I would like to use a story to communicate these ideas in more mythical or analogical form. This story will give a sense of the integrative function of the Spirit, and the need for opening to this Spirit in our time.

Spaceship Earth Today

Let's return to the Spaceship Earth story referred to in the reference to a modern creation myth earlier in this book.

Origin and Evolution of Spaceship Earth

Let's imagine that a huge spaceship containing all necessary materials for life has been orbiting a minor star called the sun in a minor galaxy. Some believe that this spaceship was fashioned by sheer blind evolutionary adaptive selection, while others believe that a guiding intelligence fashioned the spaceship. The core materials for the spaceship coalesced out of matter that originated in a primal explosion. Over billions of years one cluster of matter formed the third planet from the sun, and as it orbited the sun, an atmosphere was created that allowed the development of life, originally as particles that coalesced into atoms, then into primitive single-celled life forms. Over long periods of time, through evolutionary shifts involving the processes of complexification and emergence, this Spaceship Earth developed an amazing proliferation of plant and animal life forms. Eventually, these early life forms developed the ability to use a form of adaptive intelligence to begin to shape and influence the nature of their experience on this spaceship and thereby increase their chances of survival.

The Role of Adaptive Intelligence

Let's imagine that this process of intelligent adaptation, which took place over billions of years as the spaceship orbited the sun, was furthered in primal, collective life forms such as bacteria through their increasing ability to adapt by utilizing a primal but highly efficient collective form of intelligence.[138]

Another form of evolutionary intelligence used the mechanism of the brain to further develop the ability of animals to work together to improve their ability to survive. These adaptations fostered the evolution of an interactive dynamic of cooperative synthesis in which systems of plant and animal life fed on each other and supported each other. One chain of animal species eventually evolved into a species that utilized a relatively large and complex brain to improve its capacity for survival through toolmaking and cooperation. This species eventually developed an offshoot that we know as the hominoid branch. Over millions of years, descendants of this branch developed a brain that was capable of consciousness, curiosity, self-reflection, emotional intelligence, and altruism.[139]

The Origins of Religion

In the unfolding of this mythological story, during the early period of this evolutionary journey of the hominoid branch, their intelligence was primarily collective. There was no sense of an individual apart from the group and no thought of survival apart from the group. These early humans also experienced themselves as part of a larger realm, in which there were beings from beyond the physical level of their world that communicated with them and were involved with their lives. These early ancestors began to develop stories that gave form to their early ideas about the beings beyond—which they came to experience as gods who created their spaceship—and to develop ceremonies to worship and interact with these beings. Over time, some of these individuals were viewed as particularly gifted storytellers and seers who brought messages from the gods for all the people. Over time, these storytellers developed a collective memory of their group stories that was transmitted orally from generation to generation. Some other individuals were viewed as particularly gifted in bringing messages through dreams for the guidance of the group as well as methods of healing from the gods. In many cases, these individuals were given or discovered plant medicines for both healing and ceremonial merging with divine beings. They came to be known as shamans. (The word for this role varied in different languages, but there were similarities in this important role across cultures).

The Evolution of the Role of Nature

For most of its journey, the beings in this spaceship depended on nature as they found it. The more complex life forms developed the ability to move around to increase their access to food and other resources, and the hominoid species developed a symbiotic relationship of domestication with several animal species. The humans fed and took care of the animals, and the animals fed the humans. Most of these animals also fed on plant life. The life in the spaceship was not yet seen as something to be controlled and managed, but rather as an evolving, interactive synthesis of mutual survival.

Then one of the hominoid species developed a primal form of management of resources called herding, in which they did not just live off of hunting the animals but gathered and managed them in herds that accompanied them in their nomadic journeys to find food and explore their environment.

Another branch of the species developed the idea of managing plant and animal life into what we now call agriculture. Instead of moving where the food and other resources were, these early humans could now manage and control food, water, and shelter, with the result that they could begin to store food and stay in one place. Subsequently, they developed communities organized around this management and storage of plant and animal life. Over time, a separation developed between groups that depended on their skills in finding and hunting food and those that depended on their skills in managing, growing, and storing food, i.e. between hunter/gatherers and farmers. However, this separation was never absolute. In some locations, these groups coexisted peacefully. Some groups utilized a mixture of hunting/gathering and farming, but there were also many who chose one or the other path. In some areas, this divergence led to conflict within the spaceship over these resources.

This discovery and utilization of agriculture supported the rapid progress of culture and individual accomplishment. It allowed humans to form settlements and, eventually, city-states. However, the cost of this development of individuality and culture/technology was the loss of the primal connection with nature and with the collective. It was a loss of connection with the *Metákuye Oyás'in*, as the Lakota describe that connection, in which all beings are interrelated within a cosmic order. Instead of living off the land, people began to stake out territory they called "their" land, and the concept of individual ownership developed.

This development eventuated in increasing conflicts over land, property, and power. Eventually city-states became nations, and the wars and conflicts over property continued. Initially, these conflicts were skirmishes, but as they intensified and became wars, the collateral impact and loss of life among noncombatants increased.

In the version of this myth told by Leonard Shlain in *The Alphabet Versus the Goddess*,[140] a very significant development took place on Spaceship Earth during this era of its journey. This was the development of written language. In this version of the myth, written language accentuated the development of the left brain (the rational/logical/individual control aspect of the brain) at the expense of the right brain (holistic control of the brain) view of the spaceship journey. It also accelerated the development of a view of the relationship of masculine/feminine into one of dominance and control rather than a partnership of equality and division of labor. These developments paralleled the shift in the view of nature from knowing it as our source, the milieu in which we all live, to a view of nature that required humans to be dominating and controlling it for our own use. The serpent and the dragon—two primal symbols of the power of nature—turned from positive symbols to negative symbols.[141]

A Faustian Bargain

The Faustian bargain that evolved was that this development of written language facilitated the expansion and storage of information and technology, as well as food and other resources, that furthered our mastery and control of nature. These developments also led to the ability to exercise mastery and control over others through the accumulation of power, wealth, and resources. Unfortunately, this process of mastery and accumulation required ever greater growth and expansion. A cycle developed in which people acquired more and more but were never satisfied. Individuals amassed great wealth and empires were built out of this insatiable drive for possession and control. Indigenous people who lived in harmony with the land were often exterminated as a threat and obstacle to this development.

The Survival of Spaceship Earth Begins to Be Threatened

By the time of these developments, the spaceship had been orbiting for billions of years, but the evolution of life and individual consciousness was a relatively recent development. It led to the result that some groups within the spaceship attained the ability to significantly alter conditions for others and to destroy each other on a larger scale. Also, for these groups, religion was increasingly in service of the nation/empire, and the religious caste supported control and domination over other people rather than connection with the divine and with others.

Eventually, after a relatively short period of the total voyage, these empires had developed the need for domination to the point where wars became constant, and the insatiable ambition of the rulers led them to eliminate any threat to their power, including from members of their own families. In this culture, fathers raised their sons to be tough warriors and discouraged compassion or nurturing qualities. Boys were taught to subdue any natural compassion for the feminine or for nature. This harsh training led to great suffering, but it was thought that this suffering made them into tougher and stronger men, more prepared to fight. In this culture, life often became a survival of the fittest, which came to mean the strongest and most ruthless, leading to such an imbalance that this dominance imperative threatened constant war and destruction for the "civilized" part of the spaceship.

The Axial Age and Emergence of a New Consciousness

One perspective for understanding what happened next is the view that a higher level of consciousness intervened and effected a course correction. Axial religious figures appeared in various parts of the world that seemed to emanate a more universal and compassionate consciousness. This shift appeared to come from some new awareness that altered the direction of the spaceship for a time. Some later students of the history of the spaceship named it the Axial Age.[142] During this period, in various parts of that "civilized" world, across a period of approximately five hundred years, from the eighth to the third centuries BCE, great avatars and prophets appeared and gave messages that resonated for many people. It was stated in various forms but was similar in its core essence: Do to other people that which you would have them do to you. There was a lot more to each of their messages, but in each case the message was enhanced by the fact that these were powerful spiritual beings who seemed to speak directly from a consciousness that transcended the imbalanced view of their time.

In the region of the spaceship that we have come to inhabit, the lineage that we view as pivotal from that Axial Age for our Western history are the great prophets of the Jewish tradition, which for Christians culminated in the figure of Jesus of Nazareth.

He came from a small, insignificant part of the spaceship situated in a vast warring empire; more specifically, the dominant empire of that time—the Roman Empire. Jesus—or Jeshua as he would have been called in the common language of his time—of Nazareth embodied a challenge to that order of empire and domination. The empire, the most powerful of its time, offered order and efficiency while maintaining a policy of ruthless suppression of any threat to its control. The new vision, which Jesus called the Kingdom of God, was one in which the true ruling principle was the divine order of love and compassion for all beings rather than power and domination by one group over the other.

This Roman system of empire and domination viewed this new movement as a threat to that order, as demonstrated by the ruthless crucifixion of Jesus. However, in spite of this powerful suppression, that vision of the Kingdom of God survived and spread, initiating a new way of being in the world. Their vision was not actually totally new or unique; similar beings and consciousness shifts had emerged in slightly different forms in other areas of the spaceship and initiated in those areas a similarly more compassionate and holistic view of reality. This new consciousness embodied in Jesus was—and is—part of a larger shift in consciousness. But in that part of the world, at that time, it was a radical shift.

The Roman Empire, repeating the pattern of all empires, passed its peak. Toward the end of its reign, when it was fragmenting and decaying from within, the emperor at that historical moment in time, named Constantine, had a vision that led him to ally his empire with this new movement, known by now as Christianity. A new alliance formed, merging Christianity and the Roman Empire. This alliance completed a shift away from a holistic, integral, inclusive series of parallel accounts of the meaning and impact of Jesus to a standardized, accepted set of Gospels. Up until this time, there were many versions of the original story of Jesus, as demonstrated by the many alternate gospels recently discovered.[143]

As a result of this merging of Church and Empire, the Church became a hierarchical institution collaborating with the Empire to control and dominate through force and the ruthless punishment of anyone who deviated. It was a shift from the Way, which had been based on new forms of relationship to God and to other people that were rooted in the mystic vision of its founder and other early figures. Now it became a hierarchical system based on "right" forms of belief. In this institutionalization of right belief and conformity, survival depended on agreeing with the dominant hierarchy. In many ways, Christianity had at this point "identified with the aggressor," which is the term used for the process that happens in victims of abuse and torture if they are not able to transcend the effects of that abuse.[144] It gained the world, but lost its soul.[145]

Attempts at Course Correction

One group of Christians responded to this development by totally isolating themselves from the corrupting effects of this alliance. This was a movement of people who reacted to what they saw as the corruption of the Church by leaving the world in order to find their souls in the desert. They eventually developed into the monastic tradition that helped to maintain the soul of the Church, even as the outer structures of the Church evolved into an institutional juggernaut that destroyed everything that threatened its domination and control, including the use of forced conversions under pain of death.[146]

Having lost the original holistic vision of love and compassion for all beings based on a new order of equality for all within the Kingdom—male and female, Jew and Gentile, slave and free—the movement that had once transcended divisions became more and more divided. Christianity was not primarily responsible for the suppression of the feminine or of any group viewed as "other." However, it failed to maintain its original vision in Greek and Roman societies, increasingly adapting to a patriarchal, rational, hierarchical order based on that same hierarchical view of the known world that dominated rational thought at that time. Instead of being holistic and visionary, it became increasingly left-brain and dogmatic, built on Aristotelian logic. It continued to ruthlessly suppress any groups that refused to conform, such as a more holistic lineage in southern France. This lineage had been established, according to their tradition, by Mary Magdalene. This suppression culminated in the ruthless extermination of a group called the Cathars, who represented everything that the Church/Empire viewed as a threat to its monolithic control.[147]

In addition to this Magdalenean tradition, there was a parallel tradition (and perhaps others that are less known to us) that Neil Douglas-Klotz describes in his book *The Hidden Gospel*.[148] This lineage traces back to the versions of the Gospel story maintained by the Eastern or Syriac branches of the Church, written in their translation of the New Testament. This translation was closer to the original Aramaic that Jesus spoke than the Greek versions that the Western Church primarily used and maintained more of that holistic and integrated understanding carried in the original words of Jesus.

I could expand this story ad infinitum, but for the sake of brevity, I will summarize and condense the history leading to our present era. This brief summary could focus on so many relevant areas, but our story will focus on the role of religion and culture. (For another significant example see the new story told by Charles Eisenstein in his book *Climate: A New Story*.)[149]

As the spaceship journeyed on from the medieval to the modern world, there were always people who maintained and expanded the original vision of Christianity, the Way taught by Jesus. Many were women, such as Catherine of

Siena, Hildegarde of Bingen, Theresa of Avila, Clare of Assisi, and many other women who did not become famous. There were also Meister Eckhart, who helped restore the vision and possibility of Original Blessing, and Francis of Assisi, who, partnering with Clare, lived the integrative vision of Jesus, including all of creation in his view of redemption.

There were reformers who helped restore more integrity to the Church of their time by challenging the corruption and empire building, but these reforms also led to a further division and splintering of the larger Church. Also, the reformers were very word-based, which led to a left-brain and—eventually—more literal and theological view of Christianity. One branch of these reformers viewed success as a mark of God's favor, a sign that they were part of the elect. These Protestant cultures now took over the mantle of the Holy Roman Empire, and in the name of God, believed that because they were the chosen, the enlightened, they had the right to take whatever they wanted from others within the spaceship.[150]

The Split between Science and Religion

During this time, a huge split developed between the religious and scientific communities aboard the spaceship. There had previously been many differences in method and terminology between the religious and scientific communities, but the gap between their essential stories about the spaceship widened. Since the time of enlightenment, the religious viewpoint insisted that there was still a being outside the spaceship who had created it, given it a purpose and mission, and was still in charge of what happened everywhere in the spaceship, which was only a temporary home. The scientific community insisted that they had figured out all the mechanisms behind the origin and operation of the spaceship, and we need no longer believe that there was an outside being in charge. (This is an oversimplified description of the contrast in viewpoints, but it describes the essential differences.)[151]

The Power of the Dominator Model
and Its Threat to the Survival of Spaceship Earth

In a parallel development during this period, the political powers became adept at using both religion and science to further their attempts to control and dominate more and more of the spaceship. Consequently, the period of the journey experienced by the inhabitants as the nineteenth and twentieth centuries was marked by endless wars and empire building among the major powers. Neither religion nor science was very successful in containing these destructive wars and, in fact, often became tools in support of their own nation and its political ambitions. Once again, the unchecked ambition of the powerful elites was threatening to destroy the viability of the life forms aboard the spaceship.

Seriously out of balance, the spaceship appeared to be careening out of control. Instead of noticing the incredible danger looming ahead and doing everything within their power to prevent the destruction, the dominant powers built on the fear and anxiety of the people to try to further their own control of increasingly scarce resources plundered and then squandered by these wealthy and developed parts of the spaceship. Governments no longer focused on the development of the common good but were allied with the power of the wealthy elite, who used their wealth to control and manipulate those same governments to allow them to consolidate their shift of resources from the people to themselves. As they accumulated more power and resources, the atmosphere was burning up. Even when the instruments aboard the spaceship clearly indicated that the plundering of the earth and indiscriminate burning of fossil fuels was contaminating the atmosphere to the point where the spaceship was becoming uninhabitable, the powerful and privileged continued their pattern of insatiable accumulation.

Even when these economic megaliths became aware that their actions were poisoning and destroying the atmosphere, they remained so caught up in their need to win at any cost and to accumulate more than anyone else that they continued to manipulate the political process and media outlets to try to hide the truth from the inhabitants.

The Failures of Religion and Science

During this period, neither religion nor science was very effective in slowing or preventing this imminent approaching destruction. Much of religion was involved in total denial that the threat was even happening. These elements became more and more allied with the zealous elements of religion. According to their belief, only the ritually and religiously pure, who acted and believed in the way their interpretation of this divine being required, would be saved. Within the dominant empire of that time, the United States, this "true believer" faction united with the dominant political and economic powers to further their own control and power, even while they were themselves being used by these ruling powers to further their own interests. This "true believer" religious faction supported the economic megaliths in helping to create distrust of the scientists and engineers on the spaceship who were demonstrating that the ship's atmosphere was rapidly moving out of control.[152]

Unfortunately, science was no more effective because it was just as corrupted by the dominant powers. Although some scientists were very effective in pointing out the imminent dangers and the course corrections required, others were perfecting both the very weapons threatening to destroy the inhabited planet and newer, more effective means of plundering the planet and rendering it uninhabitable. They believed that if they simply developed their method of demonstrating the dangers and improving the tools, the masses of inhabitants of the spaceship would begin to see how irrational they had been and realize that the scientists were right. Instead of using their knowledge to demonstrate that the inevitable outcome of their way of relating to the world was leading to the destruction of the world and countering this impact by contributing to a more meaningful way of life, they concentrated on their own narrow disciplines. Like the religionists, they blamed the destructiveness furthered by their work on others and refused to take responsibility for the consequences of their actions. "True believers" in both religion and science were saying: The problem is not created by religion or science, it is created from their misuse by people who are not as enlightened as we are.

The Spaceship Is Careening Toward Destruction

It appeared to many knowledgeable people in both disciplines that the spaceship at this time was inevitably headed toward destruction. The dominant structures—political and economic as well as religious and scientific—were all caught up in their own cycles of fear of loss of power. Consequently, instead of cooperating to save the spaceship, each institution was primarily motivated by the need to dominate and control, and most of them lost sight of any larger vision or sense of the future.

The initial major threat to the survival of life aboard the spaceship was a series of confrontations between major powers aboard the spaceship during the second half of the twentieth century. One of the major powers developed weapons of mass destruction that, if used on a large scale, were capable of totally poisoning the atmosphere aboard the spaceship, These weapons then spread to other major powers. For a time, the leading scientists aboard the spaceship believed that the end of civilized life as they knew it was almost inevitable.[153]

The next series of crises facing the major civilizations within the spaceship centered on the threat to the atmosphere of the spaceship posed by the rapacious and reckless use of resources by the dominant powers. The atmosphere aboard the spaceship was heating up to the point that it was threatening the lives of many species, including humans. The resources necessary for life, such as food and water, were being hoarded and slowly poisoned by the dominant economic powers in their drive for control and domination. The more rapacious and aggressive they became, the more they feared the threat of the rapaciousness and aggression of others.

Once again, religion and science seemed more part of

the problem than the solution. The religious fundamentalists doubled down in their belief that God would intervene to either save the spaceship or destroy it and create a "heaven" in which the spaceship was no longer needed. At times they seemed bent on bringing about the destruction of the spaceship so that their God would finally intervene to destroy the world and prove them right.[154] The rational fundamentalists among the scientists insisted that there was no outside force to intervene and that we had to save ourselves by becoming more rational and more skilled in the uses of science and technology. Some of the more radical among them developed their own apocalyptic vision in which humanity would make the transition to artificial intelligence and artificial bodies, whereby material bodies would no longer be needed.[155]

Emerging Awareness of the Need for Another Axial Age

It began to be clear to the more conscious members of both the scientific and religious communities that unless we transitioned from our narrow survival of the fittest/ domination strategy, advanced life within the spaceship was doomed. Even though the spaceship itself would survive with primitive life forms, another long period of evolution would be required to re-create advanced life systems. Major die-offs had occurred before over the period of Earth's evolution when threats within and without the spacecraft had altered the trajectory of life in major ways, but this was the first one created by humans. It became more evident that whether an outside power had originated life aboard the spaceship or if it had simply evolved through natural selection, it was up to humans to resolve the situation.[156]

In the crisis 2500 years earlier that brought about the shift in trajectory known as the Axial Age, there had appeared spiritual teachers who brought expanded consciousness. They taught the necessity for love, cooperation, and compassion for all life forms aboard the spaceship. They had altered the course for a time, but it seemed that in much of our history since then religion had again allied with the dominant powers in a quest for their own institutional domination and for proving themselves right. However, in our present age it seems that rather than awaiting outside intervention, the humans aboard the spaceship would need to evolve in their own consciousness.

In the first Axial Age, no supreme God appeared to intervene in world history and punish the dominators and establish justice on earth. Rather, the change in consciousness that impacted the world occurred through the appearance of axial figures such as Buddha, the Hindu avatars, Zoroaster, and the Jewish prophets, who for Christians culminated in the figure of Jesus.

In the second Axial Age, if the shift in consciousness does occur, it will apparently not happen this time through the return of a Jesus or a Buddha or a Mohammed but rather through the commitment of their followers to bring about the return of their presence by reflecting the mind, consciousness, and actions of the founders of their religions. Those of us who grasp the reality of our situation are faced with a stark choice: transform or die! Be open to the knowing and awareness that allow us to experience the true nature of inner and outer reality. Either we reach that level of awareness or the consequence will be that much of humanity and all forms of life will have to evolve again.[157]

The Shift in Consciousness Created by the View from Space

I have included this example to give a visual and contemporary image of what I mean by holistic and integrative. This story does not mean to convey the "truth" of our history, but it does attempt to look at the entire fabric rather than the individual elements of our story. These elements are not, of course, original with me. It is, rather, a myth that has been developing in our collective consciousness for some time, particularly since the first pictures of the big blue marble we call Earth were sent back to us by the early astronauts. This image affected many of these astronauts so powerfully and deeply that their lives could no longer be the same. They were no longer just the scientists and engineers doing their skilled jobs; they had seen the true face of the spaceship we call Earth[158]

No view of religion or science today that fails to take account of this fundamental reality of our world can give us the vision we need for our time. Much of scholarly religion and rational science is still focused on the details in a very left-brain way, telling us more and more about less and less. Much of practical, institutional religion and applied science is still captive to the powers that aim to divide and control rather than helping us to see that this divide and control strategy is leading to destruction for all of us.

I do not mean to totally denigrate the value of current forms of religion and science. They still give us tools that are useful to many people in a practical way. However, if the tools are used in service of power and national interests and survival of the institutions instead of the whole of humanity, they contribute to the problem rather than to the solution.

Fortunately, there are signs that people are beginning to understand this. While the traditional powers in politics, science, and religion continue to struggle over the control of the spaceship, more people are starting to understand that the spaceship is headed for disaster, and that unless we come together to agree to change our course, we are all doomed.

Crisis and Opportunity

We stand at an important divide in our history. On one level, this crisis is manifested in the physical, material world as the inevitable result of our wars and our plundering of nature. It is a proven reality that our world and our quality of life is rapidly deteriorating. To people who look at the larger picture, it makes no sense to fight over who is in control of the spaceship Titanic, or who is right or wrong. Our instruments clearly demonstrate that unless we immediately begin to shift our course, we will face a wholesale loss of life and quality of life.

Ultimately, however, the crisis is one of consciousness, which is manifested in our relationship to outer reality. It is our consciousness that needs to change if we are to survive.

Fortunately, as the iceberg looms, more people are beginning to understand the need for a holistic response that emerges from the understanding that we are all part of the spaceship. Fortunately, pioneers and leaders in this shift of consciousness have helped us to see the world more holistically. Now even some of the leaders of our political and economic worlds are transcending narrow national and power interests to begin to work together to achieve a course correction.

An Integral View of Evolution

In addition to the impact that the view of Earth from outer space had on our consciousness, it has also been profoundly altered by the awareness that life is one integrated whole emerging in the process of evolution. No part of life can evolve without the whole of life evolving and changing. Life has evolved in a profound synthesis of synergistic whole systems within systems.

Although at the microlevel of the individual, whether human, animal, or cellular organism, there is often conflict and struggle, it has become more evident than ever through recent evolutionary knowledge that the survival of the fittest does not mean the survival of the strongest and most ruthless. The survival of the fittest means the survival of the ones who learn to cooperate, develop the capacity to nurture their young, and have the intelligence to adapt.[159]

In many ways, the system of domination and control is an aberration over the course of evolution and a one-sided development of our species. The people who are most powerful and have the most control in our spaceship today are not improving the life of the spaceship; rather, they are threatening to destroy it. Loren Eiseley, author of *The Immense Journey* and many other books about evolution, made a statement that I have been unable to locate, but which affected me profoundly many years ago. The essence of it reads something like: The hand that once lifted the axe to protect us is now the hand that threatens to destroy us. (He stated it much more poetically and pithily.)[160] In other words, while aggression and dominance were useful to individual achievement and survival, these qualities are now threatening to destroy us. Even if we view evolution as the survival of the individual gene or humans as carriers of the sexual urge to propagate life, individual survival means nothing if the individual or dominant gene survives, but the world we inhabit becomes uninhabitable for developed life.

It is also true that evolution is infinitely patient and persistent, and that if our forms of civilization are destroyed, other forms of intelligent life will emerge. The natural world does not need us to survive; in fact, humans are the greatest threat to the natural world. It is we who need the natural world if we are to survive.

The Central Question Today

The central question today is not whether we believe in God or not. It is not whether we believe in science. The question that both religion and science need to answer is: What is the fundamental nature of the reality that shapes our beliefs today, and how do these beliefs shape our actions in ways that make this spaceship an environment where there is enough consciousness to allow the spaceship to evolve and thrive rather than devolve through mass extinction? The belief that life is a blind struggle, "red in tooth and claw," in which the strongest wins was not part of Darwin's formulation of evolution. As we understand more about the complexity of the evolutionary process, it has become more evident that this description is not accurate. Unfortunately, until now this belief has been powerful enough to be used to excuse the worst aspects of selfishness and dominance. Moreover, if this belief continues to inform our view of reality, there will be little chance for the humans aboard this spaceship.[161]

The Holy Spirit Is Active Today

The origin of these ideas has little to do with my individual wisdom or capacity for originality. Another mark of the

Holy Spirit that works through all and in all is that any new transformative vision that emerges is not simply an individual vision. This is true whether we are talking about religion, art, politics, economics, dreams, or any other forms of visionary creativity. Nothing that is simply an individual creation by an individual ego has any chance of impacting the collective on a deeper level. Any truly creative act that has the power to impact a culture emerges out of the collective unconscious, which is another way to describe the activity of the Holy Spirit today. The ideas expressed in this book may seem radically new to some readers, but they emerge out of knowledge that has been present and developing for many years. They are rooted in deep knowledge of the scriptures (viewed for their essential meaning rather than as a literal description of the world). They arise out of a basic understanding of evolution and scientific reality today and out of the converging visions of religious leaders such as Pope Francis and the Dalai Lama. There is a convergence of similar ideas from many sources.[162]

The Visionary Work of Ilia Delio

One example of the unitary creative movement of the Holy Spirit is the work of Ilia Delio. Her book *The Unbearable Wholeness of Being* is an excellent synthesis of the work of Teilhard de Chardin. Delio applies Chardin's insights to our current scientific understanding of the world as well as integrating many other scholars and visionaries of the Church. Her whole book is a beautiful, well-articulated vision of where the Holy Spirit is moving us today. Her work in helping explicate and disseminate the insights of Chardin is, to me, the equivalent of the work of Thomas Huxley in popularizing and disseminating the work of Darwin. To illustrate this, I offer a paragraph from her book that expresses the essence of this section:

> To reclaim Christianity as a religion of unity is to understand its core theology in view of evolution. The Trinity is not a separate community of Persons

into which creation must fit; rather, the whole cosmotheandric process is Trinity. Love (Father) [Delio uses the word *Father*; I would say *Father/ Mother/Source*] is poured out at the heart of every being through tangential energy (Word) from which radial energy/consciousness/spirit (Spirit) is emerging. Evolution is the rise of spirit/consciousness, which means that religion is not a distinct human phenomenon but integral to the spirit of the earth ... This cosmotheandric union is creative and dynamic; it means that creation can only have one object—a universe—because the whole (God) is constantly seeking greater wholeness.[163]

This vision of a teleological (moving toward future, having a thrust toward greater complexity and wholeness) energy is what is meant by the energy of the Holy Spirit as lord and giver of life. The Holy Spirit did not just participate in the original creation, but energizes and animates the life force that moves all being toward integration. The Holy Spirit is the *Spiritus Creator* in evolution, and when we reject the concept of evolution, we reject the work of the Holy Spirit. It is, in Paul's words, the spirit that makes everything new, that is moving toward a new creation.[164]

The Sin against the Holy Spirit

In my understanding, which fits with the vision of Paul cited above, the "sin against the Holy Spirit"[165] that many people have tried to define is not a sin against some rule or precept of an outside being. The Holy Spirit works in and through us, moving us to increasing wholeness. When we resist the Holy Spirit, we resist evolution, we resist individuation, we resist the ongoing revelation of God unfolding in our time. We hold onto outmoded paradigms and institutions that are still caught in medieval views of the world. It is as though we confine God to theology and institutions instead of understanding that this God goes before us, inviting us into the fullness of this movement that is thrusting life toward complexity and integration through evolution. We do not participate in the divine energy of evolution by clinging to outmoded truths, but by trusting that this Creator Spirit has always manifested and will continue to unfold in all times and places through us—and us means all of humanity that is facilitating this divine unfolding, in the amazing complexity of revelation that is unfolding in all dimensions of our world today.

Evolution and Individuation

The microcosmic counterpart to the evolutionary understanding of the transpersonal and teleological direction of unfolding life articulated so well by Chardin and Delio is found in the concept of individuation. This is the concept that Carl Jung developed to describe the organizing principle of evolution on an individual/personal scale. He saw in his practice of depth psychoanalysis that there was a teleological drive toward wholeness and integration within each individual. Jung was the first theorist in the field of psychology to articulate the role of the Self and the natural drive toward complexity and wholeness within each person.[166]

Just as we put humanity at risk by resisting the flow of evolution, we put ourselves at risk by resisting the movement toward individuation. This is the meaning of the sin against the Holy Spirit in an individual sense. When we resist this drive toward growth and consciousness, we resist the movement of the Holy Spirit, the "lord and giver of life,"[167] in the words used in the Nicene Creed.

However, even the use of the word "sin" in this context needs a better translation and a revision in our understanding within this framework of the Spirit. In the Gospels, the Greek word for sin is *hamartia,* which is most accurately translated as "missing the mark." In other words, the Gospel of Jesus moves beyond the framework of a punishing God and into a God at work in the world today. The Kingdom of God continues to be a present reality, i.e., the active movement of divine unity and presence within our world. We can either participate in this movement toward wholeness, toward the Omega point in the processes of individuation and coevolution, or not. Whatever we understand of the meaning of God, there is no great father in the sky punishing us for not believing a particular theology or for believing the wrong thing. There is only the movement toward wholeness on the part of the individual and our entire Spaceship Earth. In my understanding of reality, this movement is guided by this central energetic presence, experienced actively as the Holy Spirit.

There Is No Punishing God, but Actions Have Consequences

Although Jesus moves us beyond a punishing God watching our every move, he does remind us that there are consequences to our choices and actions. Today these consequences are most obvious in the collective sense of our future as planet Earth. If our actions lead to our own suffering and the suffering of other beings, it is not "God" that is punishing us, it is our failure to live according to the rules of our spaceship. This Spaceship Earth has its mission set within a reality of physical laws that have been discovered in order for us to operate more effectively, as well as spiritual laws that apply to our future in the same framework of reality. If we insist on ignoring either of these sets of principles, there are consequences of our choices. These principles are the forms guiding the unfolding of the Holy Spirit, the active divine principle, in our world today. When we resist reality, we resist the Holy Spirit. We resist the evolution of life.

The Kingdom of God Is Emerging Today

However, the message of Jesus was not so much one of warning and judgment as one proclaiming the presence of the active divine lord of reality in the world of his time. This active presence of the divine in the world was continuing to move that world toward wholeness and integration, as opposed to the forces of political control and dominance that the powers of his time believed controlled the world. These same powers today, in fact, ultimately lead to the death of our developed world. Our individual death is not a tragedy; it is part of the unfolding of life. However, the needless suffering and death brought about by a world motivated by this domination and control strategy ultimately leads to the death of innocent people in the short run, and the death of much of Spaceship Earth in the long run. This devastation is not brought about by a punishing God but by the consequences of our choices and actions. The suffering caused in New Orleans and surrounding areas in the wake of Hurricane Katrina was not some arbitrary action of a punishing God for something that one small segment of humanity believes is wrong but was caused by our failure to heed the realities of natural law and the commandment to love and care for our neighbor. Instead, many people appeared to live out of this principle, which I would summarize as: "If it is happening to the poor and the marginalized, tough luck—it is their fault." We must change this level of consciousness if we are to survive.

It seems that the reality at this time in our journey is that either we become more conscious, more whole, more integrated with all of life, or more separated, more locked within an us/ them, me first strategy. This latter is the strategy of "the world," as articulated in the Gospel of John, which ultimately leads to death.[168] Jesus invites us to share, individually and collectively, in the coming of the Kingdom of God, which invites us to live out of love and compassion for all, even the least of our neighbors. Instead of dividing and conquering, we must see the presence of divine unity and compassion in all of life. This is the unitary vision and the energetic force that has the capacity to unite us to right the spaceship and restore balance and wholeness.

What Is the Necessity for Terms Like God and Holy Spirit?

Some of you may enjoy this visual image of our world today as Spaceship Earth and even agree with the conclusions, but wonder what all this has to do with the Holy Spirit, and why it is part of the theology of the Spirit.

My reading and experience, as well as the experience and

knowledge of many other people, have convinced me there is an intelligence and energy in the world today that is still active and interpenetrating with our reality, and that is what we mean by the term *God*. The term our religious tradition has used to describe this active divine energy in the world, this relational, creative presence of the divine dance within our world is the *Holy Spirit*. However, as Jesus indicated, the Spirit is not limited to one tradition or one branch of the human race. It is active throughout this Spaceship Earth and always has been active everywhere. It is a unitary presence, not divided into right/wrong, good/evil, light/dark but active in all of creation. It is the energy of dark matter as well as light. Matter and the body are also made holy by the presence of Spirit, as Teilhard de Chardin understood and celebrated.[169]

Holy Spirit and Contemporary Events

When I first wrote this section of the first draft of this book, it was the morning of November 9, 2016. Donald Trump had just become President of the United States. At that moment it was hard for many of us to believe in the presence of a Holy Spirit guiding us toward unity and wholeness when the forces of separation and blame seemed to have triumphed. That was a time to recall the Hindu concept of Shiva as creator and destroyer and of Kali as the one who clears the way within the cycles of evolution. It was also important to remember that if one were a political pundit in the world of Jeshua, and this were the morning after his crucifixion, it would have been described as an even darker time for his followers. Just when they hoped the Kingdom of God had really arrived in the presence of Jeshua, the Roman Empire had ruthlessly punished him as an example to any who dared challenge their domination and control of the known world. In Rome, this event would hardly have been noticed. In Jerusalem, the powers of institutional religion, whose primary goal was to keep Rome from experiencing any sense of threat, were merely relieved that they had rid themselves of another threat to order and stability,

We are reminded that archetypally it is often at the moment of the greatest darkness that the seeds of light are sown. It is often in the face of death, of the apparent triumph of the old order and belief in the survival of the fittest and most powerful, that new life appears. This was certainly true of the time after the crucifixion. No political pundit or historian of that time could have ever predicted that after the death of Jeshua, the new movement announcing the presence of God creating a new order in the world would grow and become a transformative movement throughout the Roman Empire and the known world.

Evolution as a Spiral Process

However, even as this transformative movement was occurring, the forces of darkness and disunity were also active in the world. The evolution of consciousness, whether collective or individual, does not move in a straight line. It operates within this world of manifestation as an alternating energy, as a spiral dance. Sometimes this energy seems to operate in an integral and synergistic manner, and sometimes one movement toward adaptation seems to dominate and create an imbalance.

So for many years after the time of Jeshua, there was unity in diversity, with many stories and gospels that presented a multifaceted interpretation and description of the meaning of this singular event. Many followers gathered around various of the early leading figures in the movement of the Way who taught differing versions of the transformative presence and power of the Creative Spirit. In the initial period after the transition from the physical presence of Jeshua to the power and presence of this Spirit, unity and synergy continued to exist between the Jewish religion that Jeshua was formed by and the new movement. The Way was a transformative new offshoot of the Jewish religion that could coexist with the old, as it did in Jerusalem. Much of this transformative energy was also found in the new rabbinical/teaching tradition that emerged after the destruction of Jerusalem and the temple.[170]

The centrality of purity and ritual was destroyed along with the temple. During the early period following the destruction of the temple, the movement led by Paul, whose mission was to the Graeco-Roman world, and the movement led by James in Jerusalem, coexisted and thrived. There was a place for the gospels of Thomas and Mary Magdalene and many others, as well as the Gospels that eventually became the only stories allowed. There was a belief in the one *Abba*, the one *Alaha*, (the words Jeshua would have used to describe this one God). The work of Neil Douglas-Klotz in *The Hidden Gospels* very powerfully describes this vision of unity in diversity present in the Aramaic consciousness underlying the early movement of the Way of Jeshua.[171]

A tragic event, the ruthless destruction of Jerusalem and the temple by the Romans in 70 CE, created the seeds of the original split that led to the separation into two distinct religions. The destruction of the temple also destroyed any belief that purity and ritual would bring about the coming of a Messiah who would create a new Jerusalem that would triumph over all earthly powers and bring about a new world order. In the aftermath of this event both the religion of Judaism and the early followers of the Way abandoned their attachment to Jerusalem and temple worship and spread into the early known world as a diaspora of both religions.[172]

The Role and Emergence of Apocalyptic Religion

The powers of Rome were then, as empire builders are now, very skilled at the strategy of divide and conquer. They found ways to get the two groups, who had coexisted and strengthened each other, to turn against each other and blame one another. A period of persecution and suffering ensued for both groups. The followers of the Way despaired again that the Roman Empire could ever be transformed, and more apocalyptic visions emerged that placed their hope in divine intervention that would create a new heaven and a new earth. They began to identify Rome as an evil power that stood in contrast to the One who would come and create this new heaven and earth. Struggling with darkness and despair, it was hard for them to believe that the Kingdom of God was present creating a new order.[173]

I am less knowledgeable about the impact of the destruction of the temple on the new rabbinic tradition that Judaism developed. What I do know from history is that this split fostered by Rome was an important element in creating the divide between the two movements that eventually led to their total separation, in which each would begin to see the other as the enemy.

It is understandable that such an apocalyptic vision would be the reaction to persecution. Apocalyptic visions emerge from despair that any real transformation can occur within this present world and the loss of hope that the active presence of the divine is at work in our present historical moment. The hope shifts to the future, and the Kingdom of God is no longer experienced as a present reality but as a future state of some other time and place.[174]

The Shadow in Evolution

At this point, I would like to introduce a concept that I believe is important in understanding this movement from unity to splitting and separation. It is the concept of the shadow, a concept articulated and developed by Jung that has become part of our current psychological discourse. Jung viewed the shadow as an archetype, i.e., something that is structurally located in both the individual and the collective human psyche.[175]

In Jung's map of the psyche, as we move from the original formless unity of birth, several psychic constellations emerge. One is the ego—the conscious organizer and integrator of our identity. Another is the self—the central organizing principle emerging out of our original unity and containing the larger and deeper organizing principle that corresponds to the outer organizing principle of the universe. This self precedes and organizes the individual person that emerges out of our unique genetic structure. As we split into conscious and unconscious states, the ego needs to adapt to the demands of the environment. In our early years, our environment is primarily formed by the parental/family values, which are shaped by family history and cultural memes to promote adaptation to the cultural and behavioral norms. In response we develop the adaptive self (also called the false self, but I prefer the more neutral term of adaptive self). Jung labeled it the *persona*—the word for the actor's mask—to describe the elements of the adaptive self that we allow the world around us to see. This adaptive self learns to conform to family and role expectations by eliminating from the conscious self all behavioral and cultural traits that are not acceptable. Two central elements of this are: those behavioral elements that are considered bad/unacceptable in the family values that have been handed down, and the gender roles and expectations mediated by the family and culture.[176]

For example, imagine a girl grows up in a family where being nice is the primary acceptable behavior. She adapts by hiding or suppressing her anger and any personal needs, instead conforming to family expectations. However, the more she adapts to these expectations, the more her assertive and natural desires become unconscious and begin to form a shadow personality that mirrors and completes the adaptive self/persona. During the developmental years, these unacceptable qualities often take the form of monsters or unnamed fears and anxieties, and constellate into a shadow counterpart to the adaptive self, the persona. These processes have been reflected in such movies as *Monsters, Inc.* and *Inside Out.*[177]

These adaptive survival patterns are part of the evolutionary individuation process that emerged as we moved from our original unity into diversity and adaptation to our environment. The ego/persona/shadow are all natural adaptive functions and are healthy when the family/environment creates a safe space for an integrated personality. However, none of us grow up in a perfectly integrated family/culture, and none of us are perfectly integrated. Nevertheless, there is an organizing principle, a life energy that moves us toward integration and wholeness on the individual and collective level.

The shadow qualities that we repress, that become

unconscious, are part of our wholeness. Often it is a life crisis that forces us to confront the fact that the adaptive self, which forms our primary defense mechanisms, no longer works the way it did when we adapted in our early life. For example, if the girl we mentioned earlier is too nice, too eager to please, she often is afraid of any natural assertiveness. This repressed assertiveness is projected onto her shadow, which turns the assertiveness into a negative quality. She may project this quality onto other girls, then onto women, and as a result of this shadow projection be afraid of strong, assertive women. It is not only men who are often afraid of strong women, but also women who have learned to repress their own strength and assertiveness. Such women have adapted by conforming to the expectations first of family and culture to be excessively nice, then often by learning to please and serve others. This adaptation tends to continue until there is a crisis, perhaps in a marriage where the spouse, out of his/her own insecurity and lack of wholeness, responds to this need to please by dominating and controlling. It is often only when this adaptation breaks down that women in such situations learn to integrate the necessary strength and assertiveness that have been relegated to the shadow.

The Shadow and Separation Consciousness

I am including this lengthy digression to give the necessary background for understanding the operation of the shadow because it is this very projection of the shadow that is responsible for so much of our division and lack of wholeness on an individual and collective level. This splitting off of shadow qualities must be reversed in the process of individuation of the individual and the collective psyche to support the integrative function of the Holy Spirit.

The most destructive historical aberrations have occurred when demagogues have succeeded by demonizing anyone who can be put in the category of *the other*, by fostering the projection of the shadow. For instance, Hitler's shadow constellated around the shame that was mediated in his family around his illegitimacy and his Jewishness. This pervasive sense of inferiority caused him to project his own shame and self-hatred onto the Jews, Gypsies, and others. We are all most susceptible to evil, to fear and hate instead of love when our fear of the other is manipulated by leaders who are themselves driven and compulsive in their need to dominate and control. As Sam Keen and others have described this process in our society, the dominant culture projects its own shadow qualities onto the group they dominate and control. This projection justifies them in their own minds in punishing and controlling the behaviors they fear in themselves by projecting them onto the Other. In our country this process happened most notably in the history of the black people we enslaved and the Native American people from whom we took this land. We projected our own aggression, repressed sexuality, and rapaciousness onto the slaves and then justified our punishing of anything resembling these qualities that they exhibited.[178]

Doris Lessing, the renowned author, eloquently describes her dawning awareness of this process in colonial Africa. She realized that the only way the colonial powers could live with their behavior toward the Africans was to demonize them and project onto them their own unconscious shadow qualities.[179] In our own empire building, we have continued to demonstrate this process of demonizing the people we control and dominate. This process, which now threatens the survival of Spaceship Earth, was demonstrated most clearly during the Cold War, when Russia and the US mutually projected their own aggressive and threatening qualities onto the other. Each massively overestimated the threat of the other and the acquisitive drive of the other. This mutual shadow projection led to the strategy of Mutual Assured Destruction, in which at a number of critical moments both sides came very close to destroying one another and much of the developed world.

When the Cold War ended, our country lacked a common, unified outer hook for our shadow, and we began projecting it onto each other. We became an increasingly divided nation in which political parties and factions tended to demonize the other. We needed new outlets for our shadow projections, so we created them. In recent years, many in our nation have found scapegoats for their projection of shadow in Muslims and immigrants, in particular. It is interesting to note how conservative/fundamentalist Christians demonize Muslims in the same way that conservative/fundamentalist Muslims demonize the West and Christianity. Each is so divided by fears and introjected judgments into good/evil aspects of Self that they are led to believe that the other needs to be exterminated to eliminate this evil shadow.

The Shadow in the Time of Jesus: Judgment versus Unity

Because this same process of projection was occurring at the time of Jesus, leading also during his time to great suffering on the part of many people, he warned us against judgment.[180] He knew from his own wholeness that judgment leads to splitting and then to more judgment. He knew that seeing the mote, the imperfection in the other and judging that imperfection leads to our lack of awareness of the log in our own eye. We project the qualities we cannot accept in ourselves and try to control them by judging them, by splitting them off. The Sermon on the Mount attempts to convey this unity—the Kingdom of God comes to all, and the sparrow is as much a part of this unity as the human. Ultimately, the ones who see this unity and operate out of love and compassion will triumph over the driven and controlling powers of the world. This vision of unity and compassion is opposed to the vision that views God as operating only with a chosen people or religion, that expects an apocalyptic intervention that will prove them right and the other wrong.

This vision inspired the early followers of the Way, but it required them to transcend their own natural tendency to project onto Jesus that vision of a Messiah who would vindicate them and punish the other.[181]

The Shadow and Splitting in the Major Religions

We see this splitting in the three major Western religions today. The visions of the fundamentalists, the religiously orthodox, are very similar in Islam, Christianity, and Judaism. Each divides the world into good/evil and demonstrates a process of mutual shadow projection and demonizing of the Other. This demonization allows Christian America to feel justified in bombing and killing innocent people to eliminate the projected evil and justify their own acquisitiveness and control. It allows fundamentalist Muslims to behead innocent people in a misguided attempt to eliminate any threat to orthodoxy. Similarly, Orthodox Jews demonize Palestinians, justifying the most extreme punishment and control methods. It is from similar views of this world as evil that apocalyptic, rapture-believing Christians are fanatically supportive of the most conservative and repressive elements of the Jewish state. Both are united in their belief that only the destruction of this world and all the unbelievers will bring about the return of the Messiah, the one who will vindicate them and punish others.[182]

The Unitary Vision of Evolutionary Religion

At this moment in our history, the visionary leaders of all three religions have a great deal in common. There are many in Judaism who have continued to articulate the message of the prophets and mystics of their tradition, who share a more unitary understanding of the One. Mohammed, from the beginning, had a vision of all three religions coexisting in his world.[183] In mystic Islam, this unitary consciousness has been maintained. In this tradition they understand that the declaration that there is nothing but the One (Allah) does not describe one right belief, but rather that nothing exists that does not express this One. This awareness of the presence of the divine throughout all being has also been maintained in mystic Judaism and Christianity and is now being understood by leaders in all three religions. This unitary vision is expressed in the work of Pope Francis, while leaders among Islam, Judaism, and Protestant Christianity are also responding to this call for a unitary vision of religion, in which the Divine Consciousness reveals itself in all times and places.

This vision also transcends the limitation of seeing Christianity as the true or superior religion. The Holy Spirit does not operate only through the Christian religion, or even only through religion. It is not only Protestant, Jewish, and Muslim leaders who understand this need for unity, but the same awareness is expressed by representatives of Buddhist, Hindu, Taoist, earth religions, and others. Spiritual leaders like the Dalai Lama, Thich Nhat Hanh, Deepak Chopra, many Hindu leaders, and Hopi prophets also understand the unitary vision toward which all of us are moving. There is no animosity toward or judgment of other religions among any of these leaders, only the understanding that there is one consciousness, which we call the One Spirit, which is uniting all religious visionaries today.[184]

The Holy Spirit Transcends Religion

This One Spirit, this wind/breath that is unlimited and free to blow wherever it wills,[185] is also active outside of and beyond any of the major religious traditions. It operates through religious visionaries who are receiving new revelations today, such as *A Course in Miracles* (to cite just one example).[186] These new visionaries are not all of equal value or clarity, but, as Jesus said, we will know their truth and validity by their capacity to produce love, joy, and peace, as well as genuine new understanding.

This One Spirit is also operating outside of and beyond any religious context. It operates through science, especially through those scientific leaders who are helping us to understand the amazingly complex and integrated nature of the physics underlying our material/phenomenal world. Scientists like Albert Einstein, Wolfgang Pauli, Niels Bohr, Stephen Hawking, Loren Eiseley, Carl Sagan, and Neil deGrasse Tyson have contributed immensely toward our understanding of the reality underlying our phenomenal world. Many other scientists share this larger, more unitary vision and are helping to birth this understanding in our world. These people, for the most part, have not viewed or described themselves as particularly religious or spiritual, but inasmuch as they help advance consciousness and awareness, they are expressions of this One Spirit.

This One Spirit also operates outside of the boundaries of religion or science, through any creative expression that advances our consciousness today. Any creative endeavor that taps deeply into the collective unconscious is an expression of this deep Spirit that moves to create more awareness and more new life in the world.[187] Some of the most prophetic and powerful vehicles of that Spirit today are poets, writers, musicians, and other artists of every genre. In our own society we see this Spirit expressed most powerfully in music that touches us deeply, whether in classical works or the music and lyrics of inspirational plays such as *The Lion King* and *Hamilton*, to cite two of many possibilities. There are very powerful movies today that can present a prophetic vision more immediately than any sermon. For me, *The Matrix* and *Avatar* are examples of such visionary movies. The *Harry Potter* series, in both book and movie forms, has had a significant effect on our consciousness.

Those who believe that the Holy Spirit is controlled and channeled only within a specific book, religion, or version of the truth are often threatened by the power of these new visions and try to demonize them as the work of the devil. However, if these works of art contribute to our greater understanding and awareness, and to the unitary movement of life and consciousness, they are vehicles of the One Spirit.

This One Spirit also transcends divisions of high and low art, or classical and popular art, or any other dichotomy. It does not operate only through art that is intellectually and artistically superior, but through any art that has a transformative and life-giving impact on the perceiver. While it is true that art that reaches deeply into the collective unconscious and facilitates an evolutionary forward momentum in our consciousness is often understood as great art, many people who may not be transformed by Bach or *Einstein on the Beach* may be transformed by the music of the Beatles, Leonard Cohen, or Bob Dylan. Others may be transformed by a country and western song that reaches deeply into the psyche, by a powerful Gospel song, or a visionary and gifted rap artist.

On the other hand, the Holy Spirit does not operate through popularity contests. In our society, much creative expression that operates to move consciousness forward is drowned by the desire to profit. These profits are achieved by cashing in on repetitive versions of what has been profitable in the past rather than by providing outlets for the creative and the new. Everything is determined by what will be accepted by the most people rather than by what elevates or inspires. Nevertheless, there are still many creative artists challenging the dominant paradigm, inspired by their creative spirit, which is an expression of the One Spirit, rather than cashing in on that which is popular.

The Unitary Movement of the One Spirit

The movement of the One Spirit is unitary, transcending the mediation of human judgment of what is good and bad in the arts, in history, in politics, and in every form of human endeavor. It is a rich tapestry of all creative forms, which in their infinite variety are capable of reaching and inspiring people at differing levels of development. These levels of development are, in the realm of the Spirit, not ranked hierarchically by intellectual or moral superiority, but by their capacity for evolving the human consciousness forward, for creating love, joy, and peace.

Ken Wilbur and Integral Theory

A powerful expression of the Spirit reaching people on multiple levels may be found in the work of Ken Wilbur and Integral Theory, which incorporates his understanding that people operate on evolving levels of consciousness. In his model, this is not a hierarchical system, but a fluid system that allows people to operate on a level that works for them, beyond categories of higher and lower levels. His model allows for a level of understanding that facilitates the work of moving beyond judgment and conflict toward an awareness that we all primarily work from differing levels of consciousness.

Evolutionary movement occurs throughout these varying levels simultaneously. We are not all capable of reaching the level of consciousness attained by Jesus or Mohammed or Buddha, or Einstein or Socrates or Pope Francis or the Dalai Lama, or the many other beings who operate on higher levels of consciousness. To paraphrase the words of Jung, we are not all called to be Jesus, but to show the same level of faithfulness to our inner calling and to the divine Self that was manifested in His life in our own lives, whatever form that calling takes.[188]

Wilbur has written a short but comprehensive introduction to this model, a book aptly named *The Integral Vision*.[189] He lays out the model and its connections to other developmental models and applies it to major human fields of endeavor, including religion. This understanding of varying levels of development helps us move beyond dichotomous and judgmental models that have characterized much of organized religion to a more unitary and complex understanding of the spiritual paths open for the unfolding of this One Spirit. This movement is not calling us to be part of one organization or spiritual path that applies to everyone, but to continue in or find the path that is right for us at our level of consciousness and circumstances. It is not up to us to judge the superiority or inferiority of any one path.

Wilbur's model helps us understand the nature of the evolving vision of the One Spirit manifesting in a pattern of unity within diversity. This unity does not inevitably eventuate in a one world government, or a single institutional religion embracing all people. Differing denominations reach people at various levels on this integral continuum, and they all play their part. There is room for the Episcopal Church and the Pentecostal Churches, to name two examples. However, there are two principles that govern the work of the One Spirit. The first is that since there is only One Spirit at work, all manifestations of the One need to understand that they supplement and complement each other. They are not called upon to judge which is the One True Religion, because there is only the One Spirit manifesting in differing forms.

The second principle is that since the One Spirit is

the energy of life and the energizing principle of reality, there cannot be a conflict between the knowledge that comes through religious understanding and the knowledge of scientific reality. Each must, as Robert Fuller states eloquently in his book *Religion and Science: A Beautiful Friendship*,[190] revise their understanding in the light of new and ongoing information/feedback. When these revisions do not occur, when "true believers" in religion or science attempt to hold on to past formulations, these beliefs intrude upon and impede the evolutionary movement of the One Spirit. When this ongoing correction through feedback from more current understanding fails to happen in religions, they become preservers of past understanding and therefore oppose the evolution of life. They are ultimately doomed to fail because attempting to hold back the evolution of new understanding is as futile as attempting to deny the reality of climate change or holding to literal beliefs in a creation story. It simply requires too much splitting and denial and inevitably results in projection of the shadow of doubt or unbelief onto others. This projection on the part of "true believers" results in demonizing others and splitting off into rigidity rather than in being a vehicle for life. When this occurs, instead of being a transformative force for a new vision of the Kingdom, it becomes a vehicle for judgment of others who do not share that specific religious view of morality or belief. Its power comes from fear; especially fear of anything challenging the old verities. It requires a belief in a punishing God who only supports those who hold on to traditional beliefs and values. It requires the ability to split our consciousness into beliefs that come from a divine source outside of this world and are often in conflict with the reality we know through science.

The Phenomenon of True Believers

We observe this split happening within the true believers found in all varieties of religious, scientific, and political fundamentalists, who become even more convinced of the validity of their beliefs when they are in conflict with reality.[191] This phenomenon has been studied extensively in social psychology, from the classic study *When Prophecy Fails*,[192] to the more recent *Mistakes Were Made (But Not by Me)*, in which authors Carol Tavris and Eliot Aronson convincingly demonstrate the human tendency to maintain our beliefs in the face of clear evidence in all major human fields of endeavor.[193] I view this book as one of the most important books today in helping us to understand how extensively our perception of reality is formed by our beliefs, even in the face of overwhelming and contrary evidence. This need to retain cognitive consistency operates not just in the fields of religion and science, but politics, economics, our judicial system, and every other major field.

The shadow and the need for cognitive consistency are rooted in a deep need that over time has evolved within humanity to protect the ego. However, although they protect the ego and are survival mechanisms, these defensive structures prevent us from being open to Spirit. A result of shadow projection is the tendency to split humanity into those who are like us—our tribe—and those who are Other, and then to see the Other as a threat to our survival. This is a behavior that Jung saw operating in the tribal structures of Africa during his visit there, but it seems to be operating even more powerfully and destructively today. We have retribalized as a defensive reaction to change and repeatedly observe in our political parties and foreign policies the belief that if our side does it, it is good; if their side does it, it is evil.

How These Two Beliefs Threaten Our Existence

One of the realities that we continue to deny today is that the more we try to kill something, the more we strengthen it. This is true for bacteria, for terrorists, and for other forms of life as well. Trying to destroy all weeds, to create a monoculture, ends up ultimately destroying the soil and the balance of nature that strengthens each element.[194] We are realizing more and more in fields from medicine to politics to psychology that we need to find a way to live in balance rather than maintaining the illusion that we can force nature to fit our version of preferred reality. If we try to kill the shadow, to continue to project it as Other, we ultimately strengthen it and weaken ourselves. The One Spirit is not only calling us to this knowledge, it is facing us with the end of life as we know it if we do not become conscious and integrate our own shadow, individually and collectively.

The other great danger to our collective survival is that tendency described above to hold on to our beliefs and constructions of reality in the face of change, evolution, and clear contrary evidence. We see this phenomenon operating in religion in the form of the true believers who are convinced that if they simply believe even more firmly, God will intervene to save them. In my reading of our religious history, it is the true believer who has often brought about destruction. True believers contrast with the great figures of religious history who, like the early disciples, came to accept that the One Spirit brings the Kingdom in its own way and time, in harmony with the unfolding of the evolutionary process rather than in response to any particular Messianic expectation. True believers of all religions are often fanatically trying to destroy others in the name of the purity and rightness of their own beliefs. In so doing, they are threatening the survival of the world.

However, it is not only or especially religion that operates out of this defensive structure. As the authors of *Mistakes Were Made* clearly delineate, this human tendency is operative in all fields of endeavor. We have recently seen it operating very clearly in the political realm, where true believers on both ends of the spectrum were certain that their beliefs were correct, even in the face of contrary evidence. Again, one of the major adaptive structures that may have once helped to solidify our group cohesiveness is now a threat to our survival.

From Splitting to Integration

The One Spirit, leading us toward unity and integration, requires us to transcend these defensive structures. We can no longer be dependent on old survival mechanisms that demonize the Other and create a split consciousness. We need to hear that inner voice, the voice of the Self, the voice of the Spirit, whether it is our internal voice or the voice of the great visionaries of our time calling us to this vision of unity and love, of synthesis and integration of the opposites.

Religions of all varieties manifest both protective responses—the tendency to demonize the other and the tendency to risk the destruction of self and world to maintain belief. On the other hand, they have also provided models of more conscious and developed beings who embody love and unity rather than fear. In Jesus, we see an example of one who called us to love all, who loved the sinner and the outsider, who proclaimed a vision of the unity of all and promised the One Spirit who would guide us toward the fulfillment of that Kingdom. This vision has often been transformative in a good way, leading to movements such as the ending of slavery, the power of forgiveness and love in the world, and the need to care for all the created world. Many today share this need to bring about a transformed world, knowing that the old ways are leading to the destruction of Spaceship Earth. Some of these are spiritual/religious leaders who operate out of faith in the possibility of transcending our old destructive ways, and some are nonreligious, or even against religion. Nevertheless, it is the One Spirit that operates throughout all life that gives the possibility of this transformative vision that could yet allow all of us to not only survive but to thrive in a cooperative and synergistic manner.[195]

This is the vision that Christianity can still offer humanity. It is not an exclusive vision or necessarily the true vision. It is one of many religious and secular paths through which the One Spirit is working. However, it is a vision that works through and with us. We are given the responsibility of healing the Spaceship Earth to allow it to survive. When we take up the vision, the One Spirit works with us to allow this vision to transform and heal. Many visionaries are leading the way, but true healing of Spaceship Earth will require all hands on deck. We will respond in many ways, emerging from our own levels of awareness and development. Regardless of the form our responses take, our survival depends on our cooperative endeavors moving toward the Omega Point that is our goal.

We Are Called and Empowered

As I have done this research and read the experiences of so many, I am increasingly convinced that in this work we are not alone. We are no longer at the childhood stage of development, in which all is controlled by an omnipotent good or bad Father. We are living in a time when the Holy Spirit, the active divine consciousness, works through each one of us. We are invited to be cocreators with the Holy Spirit. The salvation of the world will not arrive with the return of Jesus—or any savior figure—but will emerge as people take on the mind and heart of a Christ or Buddha, and bring this presence, this love and awareness, into our world. This is not a new concept. It was clearly expressed by Jesus, who said, "You are the light of the world. A town built on a hill cannot be hidden. Neither do people light a lamp and put it under a bowl. Instead they put it on its stand, and it gives light to everyone in the house. In the same way, let your light shine before others, that they may see your good deeds and glorify your Father in heaven."[196] It was expressed by Paul, who said, "In your relationships with one another, have the same mindset as Christ Jesus."[197]

It was beautifully stated by the poet Rumi in the thirteenth century. In his words (translated by Daniel Ladinsky):

> The body is like Mary and each of us has a Jesus inside.
> Who is not in labour, holy labour? Every creature is.
> See the value of true art, when the earth or a soul is in the mood to create beauty;
> for the witness might then for a moment might know,
> beyond any doubt, God is really there within,
> so innocently drawing life from us with Her umbilical universe—infinite existence . . .

though also needing to be born. Yes, God also needs
to be born!
Birth from a hand's loving touch. Birth from a song,
from a dance, breathing life into this world.
The body is like Mary, and each of us, each of us has
a Christ within.[198]

With the succinct beauty, Meister Eckhart states: "What
good is it to me that Mary gave birth to the son of God fourteen
hundred years ago, and I do not also give birth to the Son of
God in my time and in my culture? We are all meant to be
mothers of God. God is always needing to be born."[199]

The contemporary Catholic theologian Richard Rolheiser,
who combines theology and spirituality in his recent book,
Essential Spiritual Writing, continues this theme. "Rolheiser
asks us to consider the notion of ongoing incarnation. As part
of the Body of Christ, Christians carry the responsibility to be
the physical reality of God in the world. Our ordinary lives
offer the opportunity to live creatively and generatively—to
give our lives away. We are nourished in this work by prayer
that helps us reclaim an intimacy with God and fulfills our
longing to overcome our separateness."[200]

We are called to be part of a movement today toward
the evolution of consciousness in all beings, the movement
toward the Omega Point of which de Chardin speaks. In his
vision the power of love and healing represented by the Christ
consciousness empowers this movement. However, there is also
the movement toward the destruction of much of conscious life,
a movement toward disintegration fueled by selfishness, greed,
and focus on the individual ego.

The Judgment is not a singular moment outside of time, in
which some outside divine judge will pronounce our sentence. It
is an ongoing judgment that we are creating for ourselves. It is
time for all of us to see ourselves not from the perspective of "us
against them," as part of the survival of the strongest and most
ruthless, but rather as an expression of the divine consciousness
that is still manifesting as love and wholeness in our world today.
This manifestation of divine consciousness and power is also

becoming more real in our present time, despite the reality that much of organized religion has tended to codify this divine consciousness into a theology that makes it something that happened in the past or will happen in the future.

This experience of the reality of this divine consciousness is expressed clearly through the words of Aldous Huxley, who for much of his early life rebelled against religion. This rebellion was expressed in many of his early books, such as *Brave New World*.[201] In his later years, he became convinced, in part through his experiences mediated by the opening of the Doors of Perception through his entheogenic experiences, of the reality of this transcendent dimension.

I would like to quote his own description of this awareness of the reality of this divine consciousness:

> For those of us who are not congenitally the members of an organized church, who have found that humanism and nature worship are not enough... the minimum working hypothesis would seem to run about this: That there is a Godhead, Brahman, Clear Light of the Void, which is the un-manifested principle of all manifestations.
>
> That the Ground is at once transcendent and immanent. That it is possible for human beings to love, know and, from virtually, to become actually identical with the divine ground.
>
> That to achieve this unitive knowledge of the Godhead is the final end and purpose of human existence...
>
> That the more there is of self, the less there is of the Godhead, and that the Tao is therefore a way of Humility and love...[202]

I would like to conclude with a prayer that is familiar to most of us, yet translated in a way that gives it new life. This is "The Lord's Prayer," as translated from the Aramaic by Neil Douglas-Klotz.[203] As he emphasizes throughout his writing, this prayer is multi-layered, and there is no one correct translation.

O Breathing Life (Aramaic)
(an expanded, then condensed translation of Matthew 6:9–13 and Luke 11:2–4, from the Peshitta version of the Gospels)

abwun dbashmaya' (A) netqadash shmakh (B) te'te' malkuwtakh (C) nehwe' tzebyanakh 'aykana' dbashmaya' 'aph ba'r'a' (D) habwlan lachma' dsuwnqanan yawmana' (E) washbuwqlan chawbayn (wachtahayn) 'aykana' da'ph chnan shbaqn lchayabayn (F) wla' ta'lan lnesyuwna' 'ela' patzan men bisha' (G) metul diylakhihy malkuta' wchayla' wteshbuwchta' l'alam 'almiyn (H) ameyn (I)

King James Veresion: Our Father which art in heaven (A). Hallowed be thy name (B). Thy kingdom come (C). Thy will be done in earth, as it is in heaven (D). Give us this day our daily bread (E). And forgive us our debts, as we forgive our debtors (F). And lead us not into temptation, but deliver us from evil (G). For thine is the kingdom, and the power, and the glory, forever (H). Amen (I).

O Breathing Life, your name shines everywhere (A)!
Release a space to plant your presence here (B).
Envision your "I Can" now (C).
Embody your desire in every light and form (D).
Grow through us this moment's bread and wisdom (E).
Untie the knots of failure binding us,
     as we release the strands we hold of others' faults (F).
Help us not forget our source,
     yet free us from not being in the present (G).
From you arises every vision, power and song
     from gathering to gathering (H).
Amen—May our future actions grow from here (I)!

ENDNOTES

Preface

1. Gier, *God, Reason, and the Evangelicals.*
2. Tillich, *Systematic Theology.*
3. Personal communication from Dr. Kenneth Schedler, who received his doctorate in Tillich studies from the University of Marburg.
4. Twitter, Oct. 30, 2013.
5. Tillich.
6. Rom. 1:20, 4:18.
7. A philosophical tradition having a long history, popularized by Aldous Huxley in *The Perennial Philosophy.*
8. Personal communication with Dr. Kenneth Schedler.
9. Rosenthal, *Experimenter Effects in Behavioral Research.*
10. Barnes, *Athanasius and Constantine.*
11. When I was a ministerial intern, Martin Marty was a neighboring minister. He later became a distinguished professor and scholar at the University of Chicago, receiving multiple awards and honorary doctorates for his scholarship and leadership in religion and culture. Jaroslav Pelikan, an American scholar of the history of Christianity, Christian theology, and medieval intellectual history at Yale University, also received many awards.
12. Rohr, "Radical Transformation."
13. Rohr, *Falling Upward.*

God and Creation

14. For a scholarly contemporary presentation of the trinitarian nature of the divine, see Bourgeault, *The Holy Trinity and the Law of Three.*
15. Jung, *Collected Works of C. G. Jung, Volume 12.*
16. Prov. 8:2
17. This is elaborated with great scholarly insight and references by Armstrong in her book *The Bible.*
18. In Chapter 1, God creates mankind. In Chapter 3, God creates *ha adam,* which is translated as "man." Eve is from *hawwa,* the "mother of all living."

19. There is an excellent explication with diagrams in Gier.

20. Swimme, *Hidden Heart of the Cosmos*; Berry, *The Sacred Universe*; Dowd, *Thank God for Evolution*; Hubbard, *The Evolutionary Testament of Co-creation*.

21. Taylor, *An Altar in the World*; *Holy Envy*.

22. Heb. 1:1; the most radical interpretation is by Badiou, *Saint Paul*.

23. Jung, *Letters*, 375–79.

24. Gen. 1:2.

25. Gen. 1:26–27; Rohr, "You are the 'Imago Dei'."

26. Rohr, Meditation.

27. This is a fairly simplistic summary. I am not claiming to be an Old Testament scholar, although I have studied Old Testament scholarship. A good summary is found in Armstrong, *The Bible*.

28. Campbell, *The Power of Myth*.

29. Matt. 22:34–40.

30. Shlain, *The Alphabet Versus the Goddess*.

31. Quinn, *Ishmael*.

32. Gen. 3:5.

33. Gen. 4.

34. Lerner, *The Creation of Patriarchy*.

35. Kukk, "Survival of the Fittest Has Evolved."

36. Harari, *Sapiens*.

37. Armstrong, *A History of God*.

38. Ps. 51:5.

39. Fox, *Passion for Creation*.

40. Fox.

41. Rohr, *Falling Upward*.

42. Lev. 19:9–10; Deut. 24:19–22, 15:1–11

43. Dunsmuir and Gordon, "The History of Circumcision."

44. Gen. 22:17, 26:4.

45. This is emphasized in many current writings about the role of enforcers in colonization and slavery.

46. Armstrong, *The Great Transformation*.

47. Armstrong, *A History of God*.

48. Armstrong, *The Bible*.

49. Gaines, "Who Was Jezebel?"

50. Jer. 24, 25.

51. Jung, *Answer to Job*.

52. A nuanced and balanced review of the evidence may be found in Shanks, "First Person."

53. Amos.

54. Armstrong, *The Bible.*

55. Armstrong, *The Bible.*

56. This idea is expressed in Fuller, *Religion and Science.*

Jesus and Redemption

57. Jones, *Did God Kill Jesus?*

58. Many have made this point. Great scholarly exposition can be found in Pagels, *The Gnostic Gospels.*

59. These are voices that have been very relevant to me in this search. There are others who could be added

60. Cadbury, "Jesus and the Prophets."

61. Luke 17:20–21; Mark 1:14–15

62. Armstrong, *The Bible; The Lost Art of Scripture.*

63. Armstrong, *The Great Transformation.*

64. Psalm 137 is a powerful and inspired poetic expression of this struggle.

65. Shaia, *Heart and Mind.*

66. Shaia.

67. Mark 14:62; Luke 5:24, 19:10; Matt.8:20. There are many scholarly articles about the meaning of this phrase; see references in Wikipedia, "Son of Man (Christianity)."

68. Matt. 22:34–40.

69. Jefferson, *The Jefferson Bible.*

70. I later found that Bourgeault powerfully points out that Matt. 27:61 indicates that Mary Magdalene remained at the tomb with Mary, the mother of Jesus, when all the others had fled; see Bourgeault, *The Meaning of Mary Magdalene.*

71. Fredriksen, *From Jesus to Christ.*

72. This is demonstrated by Armstrong and other scholars; Armstrong, *The Bible.*

73. Acts 2:44, 4:32.

74. Mack, *The Lost Gospel.*

75. There is much scholarly controversy and little precision about dates, but there was a lengthy time of oral and Q transmission before the first Gospel was written.

76. Pagels, *The Gnostic Gospels* is an excellent source.

77. Carroll, "The Place of James in the Early Church."

78. Carroll; Acts 15 and 21.

79. The account of the crucifixion in Mark.

80. Matt. 5:17.

81. Matt. 16:1–12; see Carroll, "The Place of James in the Early Church," for more on this subject.

82. Acts 5, 22:3.

83. Acts 9.

84. Armstrong, *St. Paul.*

85. Carroll; Shaia.

86. Carroll; Shaia.

87. Alexis, *Christianity and Rabbinic Judaism.*

88. Metzger, *A Textual Commentary on the Greek New Testament*, 36.

89. Longenecker, "The Jesus of History and the Christ of Faith," provides a good summary of the scholarly approaches and his conclusions. Rohr, *Universal Christ,* provides a good framework for the current understanding of the concept of the universal Christ.

90. Rohr, *Universal Christ*; Borg, *The God We Never Knew.*

91. 1 Cor. 15:7–8.

92. Gal. 1:16; Armstrong, *St. Paul,* 28–30.

93. 2 Cor. 5:17.

94. Carroll.

95. Smith and Sweet, *Healing the Divide*; Christensen and Wittung, *Partakers of the Divine Nature.*

96. There are many people who have described this experience. They range from the advice of Carl Jung to Roland H, which was important in the founding of Alcoholics Anonymous (well described in recoveryspeakers.com: "Dr. Carl Jung Responds to Bill Wilson Letter") to many revival conversions, including that of Billy Sunday.

97. Lamott, *Grace (eventually)*; Bell, *Everything is Spiritual*; this understanding pervades all of their writing.

98. Hofmann, *LSD and the Divine Scientist.*

99. Daley, *The Hope of the Early Church.*

100. van der Walt, *John Calvin's View of the Human Being.*

101. Pope John XXIII, *Nostra Aetate.*

102. Sobel, *A More Perfect Heaven.*

103. A good review of the complex but colonial at best role of religion is found in a document from Harvard University's The Pluralism Project, entitled "First Encounters: Native Americans and Christians."

104. Power, *Sacred Wilderness.*

105. There is a sermon of this title by Jonathan Edwards, preached on July 8, 1741, that had a huge impact on American religious history.

106. Kabat-Zinn, *Coming to Our Senses.*

107. Stetzer, "A Closer Look."

108. Gustafson, *Biblical Amnesia.*

109. Sweeney, *King Josiah of Judah.*

110. See the article and bibliography on zealots at encyclopedia.com.

111. Matt. 26:31; Mark 14:27; Bourgeault, *The Meaning of Mary Magdalene*, Bourgeault points out that according to John 20:14–18, Mary Magdalene remained a faithful watcher.

112. Matt. 10; Mark 6; Luke 9.

113. Koester, *Revelation*.

114. Festinger, Riecken, and Schachter, *When Prophecy Fails*.

115. King, *Spirit of Fire*.

116. Teilhard de Chardin, *The Future of Man*.

117. Berry, *The Sacred Universe*; Swimme; Delio, *Unbearable Wholeness of Being*.

118. Tolstoy, *Kingdom of God is Within You—What Is Art?*

119. Ivereigh, *Wounded Shepherd*.

120. Pope Francis, *Laudato si'*.

121. McKibben, "The Pope and the Planet."

122. Pope Francis, "Address to Congress."

The Holy Spirit and Transformation

123. Gier.

124. 1 Cor. 13:11–12.

125. Acts 2.

126. Rom. 12:2.

127. Gen. 1:1.

128. Mark 1:10; Matt. 3:16; Luke 1:26–38.

129. 1 Cor. 15:3–8.

130. John 14:16–21.

131. Lindars, "The Persecution of Christians in John 15:18–16:4."

132. King.

133. John 3:8.

134. Teilhard de Chardin.

135. Taylor, *An Altar in the World*.

136. Merton, *Contemplative Prayer*.

137. Delio.

138. Buhner, *Plant Intelligence and the Imaginal Realm*.

139. Harari.

140. Shlain.

141. Wikipedia, "Serpent (symbolism)."

142. Originally named by Karl Jaspers in *The Origin and Goal of History*. Recently described and popularized by Armstrong in *The Great Transformation*.

143. Pagels, *The Gnostic Gospels*.

144. "Identification with the aggressor" is a defense mechanism proposed by Sandor Ferenszi and later developed by Anna Freud. It involves the victim adopting the behavior of a person who is more powerful and hostile toward them. A very good explanation of this mechanism may be found at simplypsychology.org, written by Saul McLeod under the heading Defense Mechanisms.

145. Bass, *A People's History of Christianity.*

146. Bass; Nouwen, *The Way of the Heart.*

147. Wikipedia, "Catharism."

148. Douglas-Klotz, *The Hidden Gospel.*

149. Eisenstein, *Climate: A New Story.*

150. Weber, Parsons, and Tawney, *The Protestant Ethic and the Spirit of Capitalism.*

151. Harrison, *The Territories of Science and Religion.*

152. Pies, "Inside the Minds of Trump's 'True Believers.'"

153. In 1953 the Doomsday Clock was set at two minutes until midnight after the US and the Soviet Union began testing hydrogen bombs.

154. Connelly, "Why American Evangelicals Are a Huge Base of Support for Israel." See also Lahaye and Jenkins, *Are We Living in the End Times?*

155. Ashik, *Post/Human Beings & Techno-Salvation.*

156. Kolbert, *The Sixth Extinction.*

157. See the final chapter, "The Way Forward," in *The Great Transformation* by Armstrong, as well as the messages of other conscious religious leaders today.

158. There is an excellent summary article about this phenomenon by De Luce, "Something Profound Happens when Astronauts See Earth from Space for the First Time."

159. Le Page, "Evolution Myths"; Kukk, "Survival of the Fittest Has Evolved"; Kukk, *The Compassionate Achiever.*

160. I remember this quotation from a psychedelic poster popular in the 1970s but have not been able to find it again.

161. Armstrong, *A History of God.*

162. Such as Huston Smith, Karen Armstrong, Elaine Pagels, Marcus Borg, Richard Rohr, Thich Nhat Han, and others cited in this book, as well as Pope Francis and the Dalai Lama.

163. Delio.

164. 2 Cor. 5:17.

165. Matt. 12:30–32; Mark 3:28–30; Luke 12:8–10.

166. This idea is found in many places in Jung, for example, *Psychology and Alchemy*; Singer, *Boundaries of the Soul* gives a clear understanding of this concept.

167. Nicene Creed, John 6:63.

168. John 12:31.

169. This is described in his experience in the China desert, which is described in King.

170. Frederiksen, *When Christians Were Jews.*

171. Douglas-Klotz, *The Hidden Gospel.*

172. Frederiksen, *When Christians Were Jews.*

173. Frederiksen, *When Christians Were Jews*

174. White, "Apocalyptic Literature in Judaism and Early Christianity."

175. Singer.

176. Stein, Cruz, and Buser, *Map of the Soul–Persona.*

177. Docter, Silverman, and Unkrich, *Monsters, Inc.;* Docter and Del Carmen, *Inside Out.*

178. Keen, *Faces of the Enemy.*

179. Lessing, *Under My Skin.*

180. Luke 6:37; Matt. 7:1–3.

181. Dunn, "Messianic Ideas and Their Influence on the Jesus of History."

182. Pew Research Center. "Public Sees a Future Full of Promise and Peril."

183. Armstrong, *Muhammad*

184. Taylor, "Is There a Common Ground Between Spiritual Traditions?"

185. John 3:8.

186. Schucman, *A Course in Miracles*; Williamson, *A Return to Love.*

187. Taylor, *An Altar in the World.*

188. Jung, C. G. *Psychology and Religion*, paragraphs 522 and 717; Jung and Shamdasani, 178, 189, 203, 233, 331ff, and 337ff.

189. Wilber, *The Integral Vision.*

190. Fuller, *Religion and Science.*

191. Hoffer, *The True Believer.*

192. Festinger, Riecken, and Schachter, *When Prophecy Fails.*

193. Tavris and Aronson, *Mistakes Were Made (But Not by Me).*

194. Buhner, *Plant Intelligence and the Imaginal Realm.*

195. Eisenstein, *The More Beautiful World Our Hearts Know Is Possible.*

196. Matt. 5:14–16

197. Phil. 2:5

198. Ladinsky, *Purity of Desire.*

199. Eckhart and Fox, *Passion for Creation.*

200. Greene, "Ronald Rolheiser's 'Essential Spiritual Writing' presents Christian message in all its vibrancy."

201. Huxley, *Brave New World.*

202. Huxley, "The Minimum Working Hypothesis."

203. Douglas-Klotz, *Desert Wisdom: A Nomad's Guide to Life's Big Questions from the Heart of the Native Middle East.*

REFERENCES

Alexis, Jonas E. *Christianity and Rabbinic Judaism*. Vol. 2. WestBow Press, 2013.

Armstrong, Karen. *The Great Transformation: The Beginning of Our Religious Traditions*. Anchor Books, 2007.

———. *The Bible: The Biography*. Atlantic Books, 2009.

———. *A History of God: The 4,000-Year Quest of Judaism, Christianity and Islam*. Random House Publishing Group, 2011.

———, Yuliani Liputo, A. Baiquni, and Jalaluddin Rakhmat. *Muhammad: Prophet for Our Time*. Mizan Pustaka, 2013.

———. *St. Paul: The Misunderstood Apostle*. Atlantic Books, 2015.

———. *The Lost Art of Scripture: Rescuing the Sacred Texts*. Knopf Canada, 2019.

Ashik, Mahmud. *Post/Human Beings & Techno-Salvation*. S O C R A T E S 3, no. 2, June 2015, 9–29.

Badiou, Alain, and Ray Brassier. *Saint Paul: The Foundation of Universalism*. Stanford University Press, 2003.

Barnes, Timothy David. *Athanasius and Constantius: Theology and Politics in the Constantinian Empire*. Harvard Univ. Press, 2001.

Bass, Diana Butler. *A People's History of Christianity: The Other Side of the Story*. HarperOne, 2009.

Bell, Rob. *Everything Is Spiritual: Who We Are and What We're Doing Here*. St. Martin's Essentials, 2020.

Berry, Thomas. *The Sacred Universe: Earth, Spirituality, and Religion in the Twenty-First Century*. Columbia University Press, 2009.

Borg, Marcus J. *The God We Never Knew*. Chautauqua Institution, 1997.

Bourgeault, Cynthia. *The Meaning of Mary Magdalene: Discovering the Woman at the Heart of Christianity*. Shambhala, 2010.

Bourgeault, Cynthia. *The Holy Trinity and the Law of Three: Discovering the Radical Truth at the Heart of Christianity*. Shambhala, 2013.

Buhner, Stephen Harrod. *Plant Intelligence and the Imaginal Realm: Beyond the Doors of Perception into the Dreaming Earth*. Bear & Company, 2014.

Cadbury, Henry J. "Jesus and the Prophets." *The Journal of Religion*, 5 (1925), 607–22.

Campbell, Joseph. *The Power of Myth*. Anchor Books, 1991.

Carroll, K. L. "The Place of James in the Early Church." *Bulletin of the John Rylands Library*, 44 (1961), 49–67.

Christensen, Michael J. and Jeffery A. Wittung. *Partakers of the Divine Nature: The History and Development of Deification in the Christian Traditions.* Baker Academic, 2008.

Connelly, Christopher. "Why American Evangelicals Are a Huge Base of Support for Israel." *The World*, October 24, 2016.

Daley, Brian E. *The Hope of the Early Church: A Handbook of Patristic Eschatology.* Wipf and Stock Publishers, 2002.

Delio, Ilia. *Unbearable Wholeness of Being—God, Evolution and the Power of Love.* Orbis Books, 2013.

De Luce, Ivan. "Something Profound Happens when Astronauts See Earth from Space for the First Time." *Insider,* July 16, 2019.

Docter, Pete and Ronnie Del Carmen. *Inside Out.* Animated Film. Disney Pixar, 2015.

Docter, Pete, David Silverman, and Lee Unkrich. *Monsters, Inc.* Animated film. Walt Disney and Pixar, 2001.

Douglas-Klotz, *Desert Wisdom: A Nomad's Guide to Life's Big Questions from the Heart of the Native Middle East.* ARC Books, 2011.

———. *The Hidden Gospel: Decoding the Spiritual Message of the Aramaic Jesus.* Quest Books, 1999.

Dowd, Michael. *Thank God for Evolution: How the Marriage of Science and Religion Will Transform Your Life and Our World.* Penguin Group, 2008.

Charlesworth, James Hamilton and J. Brownson. The First Princeton Symposium on Judaism and Christian Origins: The Messiah: Developments in Earliest Judaism and Christianity. Fortress Press, 1992.

Dunsmuir, W. D. and Gordon, E. M. "The History of Circumcision." *BJU International*, 83, no. 1 (1999), 1–12.

Eckhart and Matthew Fox. *Passion for Creation: Meister Eckhart's Creation Spirituality; Selections from Breakthrough.* Image, 1995.

Edwards, Jonathan. "Sinners in the Hands of an Angry God," 1741. <https://liberalarts.utexas.edu/coretexts/_files/resources/texts/1741%20Sinners%20Angry%20God.pdf>

Eisenstein, Charles. *The More Beautiful World Our Hearts Know Is Possible.* North Atlantic Books, 2013.

———. *Climate: A New Story.* North Atlantic Books, 2018.

Encyclopedia.com. "Zealots." Retrieved October 5, 1029.

Festinger, Leon, Henry W. Riecken, and Stanley Schachter. *When Prophecy Fails: A Social and Psychological Study of a Modern Group That Predicted the Destruction of the World.* Wilder Publications, 2018.

Fox, Matthew. *Passion for Creation: The Earth-Honoring Spirituality of Meister Eckhart.* Inner Traditions, 2000.

Fredriksen, Paula. *From Jesus to Christ: The Origins of the New Testament Images of Jesus.* Yale University Press, 2000.

———. *When Christians were Jews.* Yale University Press, 2018.

Fuller, Robert W. *Religion and Science: A Beautiful Friendship?* CreateSpace, 2012.

Gaines, Janet Howe. "Who was Jezebel?" *Bible History Daily,* November 9, 2019.

Gier, Nicholas F. *God, Reason, and the Evangelicals: The Case against Evangelical Rationalism.* University Press of America, 1987.

Giridharadas, Anand. *Winners Take All: The Elite Charade of Changing the World.* Vintage Books, 2019.

Greene, Dana. "Ronald Rolheiser's 'Essential Spiritual Writing' Presents Christian Message in all Its Vibrancy." *National Catholic Reporter.* January 29, 2022.

Gustafson, Scott W. *Biblical Amnesia: A Forgotten Story of Redemption, Resistance and Renewal.* Infinity, 2004.

Harari, Yuval N. *Sapiens: A Brief History of Humankind.* McClelland & Stewart, 2014

Harrison, Peter. *The Territories of Science and Religion.* University of Chicago Press, 2015.

Hoffer, Eric. *The True Believer.* Harper & Row, 1951.

Hofmann, Albert, Christian Rätsch, and Alex Grey. *LSD and the Divine Scientist: The Final Ghoughts and Reflections of Albert Hofmann.* Park Street Press, 2013.

Hubbard, Barbara Marx and Neale Donald Walsch. *The Evolutionary Testament of Co-Creation: The Promise Will Be Kept.* Muse Harbor Publishing, 2015.

Huxley, Aldous. *Brave New World.* Vintage, 1932.

———. "The Minimum Working Hypothesis." In Aldous Huxley and Jacqueline Hazard, *The Divine Within: Selected Writings on Enlightenment.* HarperPerennial, 2013.

———. *The Perennial Philosophy.* Chatto & Windus, 1946.

Ivereigh, Austen. *Wounded Shepherd: Pope Francis and His Struggle to Convert the Catholic Church.* Henry Holt and Company, 2019.

Jaspers, Karl and Michael Bullock. *The Origin and Goal of History.* New Yale University press, 1953.

Jefferson, Thomas. *The Jefferson Bible: The Life and Morals of Jesus of Nazareth.* Beacon Press, 1989.

LaHaye, Tim and Jerry B. Jenkins, *Are We Living in the End Times?* Tyndale House Publishers, 1999.

Jones, Tony. *Did God Kill Jesus? Searching for Love in History's Most Famous Execution.* Harper One, 2015.

Jung, Carl Gustav. *Psychology and Alchemy*. Pantheon Books, 1953.

———. *Psychology and Religion*. Yale University Press, 1938.

Jung, Carl Gustav and Gerhard Adler. *Letters, Vol. 2, 1951–1961*. Routledge, 1976.

Jung, Carl Gustav and Sonu Shamdasani. *Answer to Job*. Princeton University Press, 2010.

———. *The Red Book = Liber Novus: A Reader's Edition*. W.W. Norton, 2012.

Kabat-Zinn, Jon. *Coming to Our Senses: Healing Ourselves and the World Through Mindfulness*. Hyperion, 2005.

Keen, Sam. *Faces of the Enemy: Reflections of the Hostile Imagination*. Harper & Row, 1991.

King, Ursula. *Spirit of Fire: The Life and Vision of Pierre Teilhard De Chardin*. Orbis Books, 2015.

Koester, Craig R. *Revelation: A New Translation with Introduction and Commentary*. Yale University Press, 2014.

Kolbert, Elizabeth. *The Sixth Extinction: An Unnatural History*. Bloomsbury, 2014.

Kukk, Christopher. "Survival of the Fittest Has Evolved: Try Survival of the Kindest." *Better by Today,* March 7, 2017.

Kukk, Christopher. *The Compassionate Achiever: How Helping Others Fuels Success*. HarperOne, 2017.

Lamott, Anne. *Grace (eventually): Thoughts on Faith*. Penguin Group, 2007.

Le Page, Michael. "Evolution Myths: 'Survival of the Fittest' Justifies 'Everyone for Themselves.'" *NewScientist,* April 16, 2008.

Lerner, Gerda. *The Creation of Patriarchy*. Oxford University Press, 1986.

Lessing, Doris. *Under My Skin: Volume One of My Autobiography*. HarperCollins, 1994.

Lindars, B. "The Persecution of Christians in John 15:18–16:4." In *Suffering and Martyrdom in the New Testament,* edited by William A. Horbury and Brian McNeil. Cambridge University Press, 2011.

Longenecker, Richard N. "The Jesus of History and the Christ of Faith: Some Contemporary Reflections." Lecture given at the Yorkminster Park Theological Forum, Toronto, February 11, 1999.

Mack, Burton L. *The Lost Gospel: The Book of Q and Christian Origins*. Element, 1994.

McKibben, Bill. "The Pope and the Planet." *The New York Review of Books* 13 (April 13, 2015), 40–42.

McLeod, Saul. "Defense mechanisms." simplypsychology.org, 2019. <https://www.simplypsychology.org/simplypsychology.org-Defense-Mechanisms.pdf>

Merton, Thomas. *Contemplative Prayer*. Image Books, 1971.

Metzger, Bruce Manning. *A Textual Commentary on the Greek New*

Testament. Deutsche Bibelgesellschaft, 1994.

Nouwen, Henri J. M. *The Way of the Heart*. The Seabury Press, 1981.

Pagels, Elaine H. *The Gnostic Gospels*. Vintage Books, 1989.

———. *The Origin of Satan*. Vintage Books, 1996.

Pew Research Center. "Public Sees a Future Full of Promise and Peril." *Life in 2050: Amazing Science, Familiar Threats,* June 22, 2010.

Pies, Ronald W. "Inside the Minds of Trump's 'True Believers.'" *The Conversation,* July 11, 2017.

The Pluralism Project. *First Encounters: Native Americans and Christians*. Harvard University, 2020.

Pope Francis. *Laudato si': On Care for Our Common Home*. Encyclical Letter. May 24, 2015.

Pope Francis. "Address to Congress." McClatchy Washington Bureau. September 24, 2015.

Pope John XXIII. *Nostra Aetate*. October 28, 1965.

Power, Susan. *Sacred Wilderness*. Michigan State University Press: 2014.

Quinn, Daniel. *Ishmael*. Bantam Books, 1992.

Rohr, Richard. *Falling Upward: A Spirituality for the Two Halves of Life*. John Wiley & Sons, Inc., 2011.

———. Meditation. Center for Action and Contemplation, October 14, 2014.

———. "Radical Transformation" Meditation. Center for Action and Contemplation. May 12, 2016.

———. *The Universal Christ: How a Forgotten Reality Can Change Everything We See, Hope For, and Believe*. Convergent Books, 2019.

———. "You are the 'Imago Dei,'" Meditation. Center for Action and Contemplation. June 20, 2018.

Rolheiser, Ronald. *Essential Spiritual Writings*. Orbis, 2021.

Rosenthal, Robert. *Experimenter Effects in Behavioral Research*. Wiley, 1976.

Schucman, Helen. *A Course in Miracles*. Course in Miracles Society, 1972.

Shaia, Alexander J. *Heart and Mind: The Four Gospel Journey for Radical Transformation*, edited by Michelle L. Gaugy. Journey of Quadratos, 2017.

Shanks, Hershel. "First Person: Did the Kingdoms of Saul, David, and Solomon Actually Exist?" *Bible History Daily,* December 21, 2019.

Shlain, Leonard. *The Alphabet Versus the Goddess: The Conflict between Word and Image*. Penguin, 2000.

Singer, June. *Boundaries of the Soul: The Practice of Jung's Psychology*. Doubleday, 1972.

Smith, Amos and Leonard Sweet. *Healing the Divide: Recovering Christianity's Mystic Roots*. Wipf and Stock Publishers, 2013.

Smith, Huston and Jeffery Paine. *Tales of Wonder: Adventures Chasing the Divine*. HarperOne/HarperCollins Publishers, 2009.

Sobel, Dava. *A More Perfect Heaven: How Copernicus Revolutionized the Cosmos.* Bloomsbury, 2011.

Stein, Murray, Leonard Cruz, and Steven Buser. *Map of the Soul: Persona: Our Many Faces.* Chiron Publications, 2019.

Stetzer, E. "A Closer Look: Messianic Expectations." *Christianity Today,* March 7, 2012.

Sweeney, Marvin A. *King Josiah of Judah The Lost Messiah of Israel.* Oxford University Press, 2001.

Swimme, Brian. *Hidden Heart of the Cosmos: Humanity and the New Story.* Orbis Books, 2019.

Tavris, Carol, and Elliot Aronson. *Mistakes Were Made (But Not by Me): Why We Justify Foolish Beliefs, Bad Decisions and Hurtful Acts.* Pinter & Martin, 2020.

Taylor, Barbara Brown. *An Altar in the World: A Geography of Faith.* HarperOne, 2010.

Taylor, Barbara Brown. *Holy Envy: Finding God in the Faith of Others.* Canterbury Press, 2019.

Taylor, Steve. "Is There a Common Ground Between Spiritual Traditions?" *Psychology Today,* March 1, 2019.

Teilhard de Chardin, Pierre. *The Future of Man.* Harper & Row, 1969.

———. *The Phenomenon of Man.* Collins, 1959.

Teilhard de Chardin, Pierre, and René Hague. *Christianity and Evolution.* Harcourt, Inc, 2002.

Tillich, Paul. *Systematic Theology.* Chicago: University of Chicago Press: 1967.

Tolstoy, Count Leo Nikolayevich. *Kingdom of God Is Within You—What Is Art?* Outlook Verlag, 2018.

van der Walt, B. J. "John Calvin's View of the Human Being: A Christian Philosophical Appraisal." *Tydskrift vir Geesteswetenskappe* 49, no. 3 (2009), 365-396.

Weber, Max, Talcott Parsons, and R. H. Tawney. *The Protestant Ethic and the Spirit of Capitalism.* Wilder Publications, 2010.

White, L. Michael. "Apocalyptic Literature in Judaism and Early Christianity." <https://www.pbs.org/wgbh/pages/frontline/shows/apocalypse/primary/white.html>

Wikipedia. "Catharism." Retrieved August 30, 2020.

———. "Serpent (symbolism)." Retrieved August 30, 2020.

———. "Son of man (Christianity)." Retrieved August 25, 2020.

———. "Relationship between religion and science." Retrieved August 29, 2020.

Wilber, Ken. *The Integral Vision: A Very Short Introduction.* Shambhala, 2018.

Williamson, Marianne. *A Return to Love: Reflections on the Principles of "A Course in Miracles."* HarperOne, 1996.

ABOUT THE AUTHOR

 Harvey H. Honig is a former Jungian Analyst/Psychologist who retired after decades of private practice and teaching in order to answer the call to write this book. He spent five years as a Lutheran minister before moving to Chicago to begin analysis with June Singer and training as an analyst while earning a Ph.D. in Psychology from Loyola University of Chicago. He also received a Masters in Divinity from Concordia Seminary in St. Louis, and an STM in Pastoral Counseling at Oberlin School of Theology. He was in private practice in Madison, Wisconsin, where he still lives with his wife, Jean. He is also author of the chapter "Inner Dialogue and the Psychology of Carl Jung" in the book *Inner Dialogue in Daily Life*.

SHANTI ARTS

NATURE · ART · SPIRIT

Please visit us online
to browse our entire book catalog,
including poetry collections and fiction,
books on travel, nature, healing, art,
photography, and more.

Also take a look at our highly regarded art
and literary journal, *Still Point Arts Quarterly*,
which may be downloaded for free.

www.shantiarts.com

CPSIA information can be obtained
at www.ICGtesting.com
Printed in the USA
LVHW101907210622
721764LV00008B/906